"TO SHOW ...
BEYOND THE ...
THEY ARE STAN...
TIC THING"

—Robert Altman

Each film of Robert Altman is an unforgettable trip into a new and different world.

It may be a world of war both hellish and comic . . . a world shadowed by mystery and haunted by terror . . . a world where country music and national politics come crushingly together . . . a world of Depression love and violence . . . a world of the wild and not so wonderful west . . . a world of a pair of compulsive gamblers out to beat the odds . . . a world of a down-at-his-heels detective in a maze of monstrous corruption . . . a world of a wedding that becomes a microcosm of American society . . .

This book offers you a complete tour of that world—and a portrait-in-depth of the man who has created it.

It is a journey no movie lover will want to miss.

Edited by Leonard Maltin, and available in Popular Library editions:

HOLLYWOOD: THE MOVIE FACTORY

Oversized Books in Popular Library's Big Apple Film Series:

HOLLYWOOD CORRAL   08443-X $3.95

ROBERT REDFORD   08412-X $3.95

ABBOTT AND COSTELLO   08372-7 $3.95

TEX AVERY: King of Cartoons   08396-4 $3.95

STANLEY KUBRICK A FILM ODYSSEY

08414-6 $3.95

SUPERMAN   08459-6 $4.95

And now available in rack size:

ABBOTT AND COSTELLO   04138-2 $2.25

STANLEY KUBRICK   A FILM ODYSSEY

04101-3 $2.25

SUPERMAN   04054-8 $1.95

ROBERT ALTMAN:

AMERICAN INNOVATOR

by Judith M. Kass

Popular Library Film Series
Leonard Maltin, General Editor

POPULAR LIBRARY · NEW YORK

ROBERT ALTMAN: AMERICAN INNOVATOR

Published by Popular Library, a unit of CBS Publications, the Consumer Publishing Division of CBS Inc.

Copyright © 1978 by Leonard Maltin

ISBN: 0-445-04262-1

Photograph credits and acknowledgments: United Artists, Warner Brothers, Commonwealth United Entertainment, Twentieth Century-Fox, Metro-Goldwyn-Mayer, Columbia Pictures, Paramount Pictures, Museum of Modern Art Film/Stills Archive.

We welcome your thoughts and comments on this book. Address all correspondence to Leonard Maltin, General Editor, 200 West 79 Street, New York, New York 10024.

Printed in the United States of America

10 9 8 7 6 5 4 3 2 1

Acknowledgments

My deepest thanks to Mike Donatio, Jon Gartenberg, Jeff Schulman, Emily Sieger, and Charles Silver of the Museum of Modern Art Film Department; Joseph Balian and Barbara J. Humphrys of the Library of Congress; and Jim D'Anna.

Special thanks are due Michael Murphy for his insights and observations, as recorded in an interview with Leonard Maltin.

TABLE OF CONTENTS

Introduction:
Robert Altman and His Films

"I have nothing to say, nothing to preach. It's just painting what I see. . . . To show people something beyond the scope of where they are standing is a fantastic thing."

If Robert Altman had nothing to say in the cinema, he'd still, presumably, be tattooing ID numbers on dogs' thighs for a living, or making industrial films in Kansas City. It is impossible not to believe that Altman wants very much for people to understand what he's doing cinematically; he just wants people to make an investment in his films—to see them emotionally, rather than intellectually. As Altman has said, his perfect film would be one which, after seeing, the audience would be unable to talk about. The mere fact that Altman struggles so hard to make the films *he* wants to make, that he doesn't make Charles Bronson epics for the money, is a demonstration of his commitment to his idea of film.

Robert Altman was born February 20, 1925, in Kansas City, Missouri. His father was one of the most successful life insurance salesmen in the world. He was also an inveterate gambler, and his son says: "I learned a lot about losing from him. Losing is an identity; you can be a good loser and a bad winner; none of it—gambling, money, winning or losing has any real value; it's simply a way of killing time, like crossword puzzles."

Altman was educated in Jesuit schools and raised as a Roman Catholic. He left the church about the same time as he joined the army in 1943. He was a B-54 bomber pilot and flew forty-six missions over Borneo and the Dutch East Indies. Discharged from the army in 1947, he attended the University of Missouri, then began making industrial films for the Calvin Company in Kansas City. He was a writer, photographer, producer, set designer, director, and film editor.

Asked years later to explain his motivation for going into the film business, he answered: "I don't know. I failed with everything else. I think I was originally attracted by the glamor and the adulation, and I thought I would be able to date Gloria DeHaven—all this. You know, Jack Kennedy didn't wake up and say, 'I want to be President.' People don't do that. You start walking."

In 1948 he coauthored a story with George W. George that was produced by RKO as *Bodyguard*, and in the 1950s he went to Hollywood with his cameraman Lou Lombardo, hoping to get a toehold, but was unsuccessful and returned to Kansas City. In 1955 he was approached by a local backer to make a feature film; the only stipulation was that it had to be about juvenile delinquents. Altman obligingly wrote, directed, produced, and drove the generator truck for *The Delinquents*, which got mediocre reviews when United Artists finally released it in 1957. Altman has succeeded in rounding up most existing prints and refuses to show the film to anyone.

Altman married almost as soon as he returned from World War II—the last girl he'd known before leaving, Lavonne Elmer. The marriage was a disaster. Altman's comment is: "I was a real chippie chaser." By his first union, Altman had a daughter, Christine, now twenty-

Altman on the set of BREWSTER McCLOUD

nine. His second marriage, to Lotus Corelli, produced two sons, Michael, twenty-two, and Stephen, nineteen. He has married a third time, to a calm, lovely woman named Kathryn. The Altmans have a son, Bobby, and have adopted a second, Matthew.

Warner Brothers hired Altman to make *The James Dean Story* in 1957. It is a compilation documentary with a doom-laden, sepulchral narration read by Martin Gabel, apparently through a foghorn. But it served to get Altman noticed by Alfred Hitchcock, who hired him to direct some episodes of the TV series *Alfred Hitchcock Presents*. Altman's television career was launched. Although he was steadily employed from 1957 to the mid-sixties, his path was strewn with the controversy that has marked his career in films, mostly over his penchant for having more than one voice on the sound track at the same time. Altman directed segments of *The Roaring Twenties*, *Bonanza*, *Combat*, *Bus Stop*, *Suspense Theatre*, *Kraft Theater*, *Whirlybirds*, *The Millionaire*, and *Kraft Mystery Theater*, as well as the pilots for *The Gallant Men* and *The Long Hot Summer*. Michael Murphy, who worked with Altman quite a lot in those days, recalls, "Every studio in town fired him, at one time or another; in general it had a lot to do with the sound. In *Combat* we were all talking on the same track."

As Altman told Aljean Harmetz of the *New York Times*, "Because the star of *Combat*, Vic Morrow, couldn't be killed off, I'd take an actor, establish him as an important character in one segment, use him three or four times more, and then kill him early in the next script, offscreen, in a way that had nothing to do with the plot. That was unorthodox. It made them nervous. I used to get fired for it."

One of Altman's TV episodes (for Kraft Suspense

Altman directs McCABE AND MRS. MILLER on location in Vancouver

Theater) became a TV movie, the 1964 *Nightmare in Chicago*, which portrayed detective Charles McGraw trailing a killer nicknamed Georgie Porgie around that city.

When he was making $125,000 a year from television, Altman quit because he was afraid of becoming "one of those hundreds of creative people who have just died on television." He was mostly unemployed until 1966, when he did a programmer for Jack Warner called *Countdown*. He was fired from the project for the same old problem: More than one actor could be heard on the soundtrack at the same time.

Having no income didn't encourage him to give up his favorite pastime, gambling, or spending a thousand dollars for clothes just to cheer himself up. He was considered such a bad risk that he didn't get an American Express card until December of 1970. He dropped four hundred dollars to Arthur Kopit playing backgammon when Kopit visited the location of *Buffalo Bill and the Indians*, and he regularly takes fliers on football games. But mostly Altman gambles on his films, on making each one different from the one that preceded it and on trusting his luck that the public which likes one film will accept it when he veers off on an entirely different tack for the next movie.

One method Altman has adopted to insure that his luck, insofar as he can control it, will remain constant, is to repeatedly cast actors he works well with in his films. The first such member of the so-called repertory company was Michael Murphy, who has made five films with Altman and who says, "So far as that 'stock company' identification is concerned, I think it makes good copy and all that, but in reality, we're just good friends and it's fun. It's been turned into kind of an elitist thing, which it really isn't, I don't think. I never hustle him for a job. I never feel left out of a picture if he doesn't give me a part, although I've been in all the good ones. Been in all the *better* ones. He ought to get that message by now—Bob."

Barbara Baxley made *Countdown* and *Nashville* with Altman, and introduced him to Sandy Dennis, who starred in *That Cold Day in the Park* for him. Elliott Gould starred in *M*A*S*H*, *The Long Goodbye*, and *California Split*. Shelley Duvall made *Brewster McCloud*, *McCabe and Mrs. Miller*, *Thieves Like Us*, *Nashville*, *Buffalo Bill and the Indians*, and *3 Women*. René Auberjonois did *M*A*S*H*, *Brewster McCloud*, *McCabe and Mrs. Miller*, and *Images* for Altman. Bert Remsen was a casting director on *Brewster* when Altman

cast him as Breen; he went on to make four more films for
the director. Geraldine Chaplin appeared in *Nashville*,
then *Buffalo Bill*, and went on to make *Welcome to L.A.*,
the first film directed by Alan Rudolph, who was
Altman's coauthor on *Buffalo Bill*. Lily Tomlin made
Nashville for Altman, then did *The Late Show*, which he
produced and Robert Benton directed.

Keith Carradine has made three films with Altman and
starred in *Welcome to L.A.* for Rudolph. John Considine
had a small part in *California Split*, then larger roles in
Buffalo Bill, *L.A.*, and *The Late Show*, and, with Altman,
wrote the script for *A Wedding*, in which he plays a
security officer. Julie Christie and Elliott Gould, stars
from earlier films, "dropped in" to play themselves in
Nashville, and Joan Tewkesbury, the coauthor of the
script, played the woman at the train station who talks to
Shelley Duvall in *Thieves Like Us*.

Along with the notion of a "repertory company" is the
idea of "behaviors," as Altman likes to call his actors,
performers whose range he is familiar with and whose
style is such that, although he may use them differently in
each film (Keith Carradine played a virginal bank robber
in *Thieves Like Us*, then a priapic rock star in *Nashville*),
he knows what they are capable of. And this leads to the
question of improvisation, a technique that Altman
doesn't use literally, but which he feels comfortable with.
As Altman describes working on *Nashville*: "The
improvisation part of it usually is the rehearsal.
Throughout this picture with Geraldine Chaplin, most of
her stuff we didn't set at all. She attacked each character
as she knew the character was, and we let those interviews
run on." Speaking on Ned Beatty and his "behavior" in
the same film, Altman said, "I have always had control of
the casting of my films. We just cast a film the way we

think. I don't feel I have a rep company—but take an actor like Ned Beatty, for instance. Say I didn't make *Nashville*. I'm going to sit and say, 'Oh, that guy's very good for this kind of thing.' I may eliminate him from six or seven other possibilities, but working with him and seeing how he works with other people, you start to see the range of the actor. I just have more knowledge of the range of these actors than a director who hasn't worked with them. It's comfortable to know that you've got somebody that you can communicate with, and who understands what you're doing or at least responds to it. It's fun to see people in three or four different pictures really do different things and do them well."

Michael Murphy describes Altman's method of working on a film: "He's like a host at a party. *Nashville* was supposed to start on the fifteenth of July, but everyone had to be [in Nashville] on the fourth of July 'cause he was having a party. So we went down there and we went to his party. He took us around and everyone got to know one another, and our relationships kind of developed as the picture developed. And that's the way he directs." Murphy talks about the character he plays in *Nashville*, advance man John Triplette: "There are several layers to the character that weren't in the script, and an awful lot of that happened just on the spur of the moment. It came out of a lot of scenes that we improvised and played with and talked about, and a lot of just thinking about these characters. And having the latitude to explore different areas of his being. I think my performances have become better and better in his movies because I'm more and more comfortable with [Altman] and around him."

Another form of improvisation takes place in *3 Women*, a process Altman relates by saying, "Nothing

Altman and Paul Newman working on BUFFALO BILL

changed the story line. Shelley did a lot of her monologues and the diary. I would write a monologue for her about something, and she'd say, 'Well, can't I do this myself?' and I'd say, 'Yeah, I just want to add a line of it.' So she really wrote maybe twenty of those monologues. She'd say, 'I think I'll use this one.' She would take the events that happened, and she constructed the language that was in the diary because she wrote it herself." In another context Altman referred to this procedure: "Neither Sissy Spacek nor Shelley can improvise in the strict sense of the term. They need the lines to speak before the cameras begin turning. They contributed dialogue and shaped their own characters in a lot of ways, but none of it was improvised in front of the camera. I had the first thirty-five pages of the screenplay written by the time we started. But then by the time we had shot the first week, I knew a lot more about those two characters. So then I would do the next scene, and they would draw on things that had already happened. We shot it in sequence."

Robert Benton, the director of *The Late Show*, reports a conversation he had with Altman when he was feeling apprehensive about his producer's working methods. "I told him I didn't think I'd be able to improvise, and he was startled. 'I don't improvise,' he said. 'I just rewrite later than you do.'" Altman says, "It's true. I prefer to get up early in the morning to write the final dialogue for that day's scenes. It's not improvisation. It's just a technique for keeping the working process as spontaneous as possible."

Altman's production company, Lion's Gate Films, has developed a number of talented people whom Altman has difficulty keeping steadily employed on films that he directs. One method of retaining their services is to produce films that he doesn't direct. *Welcome to L.A.* and *The Late Show* are the first of these films. Leon Ericksen was the art director for *Brewster*, *McCabe*, and *California Split*, and on *M*A*S*H* he was the associate producer. Robert Eggenweiler has been Altman's associate producer for *That Cold Day in the Park* and all the films from *Brewster* to the present. Tommy Thompson has been the assistant director of five Altman films, and Paul Lohmann has photographed three of them. Lou Lombardo has been the editor of *Brewster*, *McCabe*, *Thieves Like Us*, *The Long Goodbye*, and *California Split*. Maysie Hoy played the Chinese prostitute in *McCabe and Mrs. Miller* and one of Shelley Duvall's cotherapists at the spa in *3 Women*. She was also an assistant editor on the latter film and a production assistant on *Nashville*. There are several more cases of technical personnel whose careers are wound around that of Robert Altman.

Another device Altman uses to keep the film "in the family," so to speak, is to assign the names of people working on the film to characters in the film or to let them use their own names. Jo Ann Brody played Jo Ann Eggenweiler, Mark Rydell's mistress, in *The Long Goodbye*. Sybil Scotford played Mrs. Tewkesbury, the name of Altman's scriptwriter on *Thieves Like Us* and *Nashville*. Assigning a mixture of the five actors' names to the characters in *Images* is another example of Altman's simplification.

Altman likes show-business motifs, which appear regularly in his films, or bits of activity related to shows, and this derives, at least partly, from being comfortable with his performers. Donald Sutherland's and Elliott Gould's behavior in *M*A*S*H* is a show in itself— theatrical, mannered, and even artificial in its heightened, cool relaxation. And there's the spoof of John Schuck's "suicide," a play in itself, complete with music and a grand finale. *Brewster McCloud* takes place at the Houston Astrodome, an arena devoted not only to sports but to shows as well. The rehearsal that opens the film, with its costumes and music, is part of a spectacle, as is the finale, with its circus theme and bows for the performers, who are introduced by their real names, a technique borrowed from the previous film, *M*A*S*H*. And of course both films, in using this device, call attention to themselves as movies; *Brewster* goes even further by repeating part of the opening credits as the band repeats its rendition of "The Star Spangled Banner." Warren Beatty's behavior at the beginning of *McCabe and Mrs. Miller* is a kind of show, as he tries to impress the inhabitants of Presbyterian Church with his city ways, his tablecloth, his diamond stickpin, and his bowler hat, and he's planning another form of show, a gambling joint and whorehouse, where women and money will be the chief items on display.

In *The Long Goodbye*, the conduct of the three male protagonists (Gould, Sterling Hayden, and Mark Rydell) is a species of theater, with their respective affectations: Gould's deceptive laid-back casualness, Hayden's bluff deterioration, and Rydell's hopped-up hostility. Altman uses 1930s radio shows in *Thieves Like Us* to comment on the action and heighten the drama of what is taking place on screen, and the semi-hysteria of John Schuck's performance is a kind of show in itself, with its broad theatrical gestures, its rages, and its trumpeting, bravura style. Both Gould and George Segal, especially Gould, do *shtick*, a species of exhibitionism, in *California Split*, and the film opens with a mini-movie on how to play poker. The ending, in a Reno gambling palace, has its own allusions to show business in the gaudy decorating mode of the casino and the stylized actions of many of its denizens.

Nashville is almost all show, its most obvious point of methodology being to demonstrate the relationship between show business and politics. Henry Gibson is almost always performing, in his role as a country-and-western star, whether he's literally singing or mouthing his glowing banalities about the Nashville way of life and giving his son the opportunities he never had. The characters of *Buffalo Bill and the Indians* are literally on stage for at least half the movie, and when they're off they're performing anyway, whether it's in the form of Paul Newman's theatrical carrying on, Kevin McCarthy's flamboyant personal and prose style, or Joel Grey's self-conscious pomposity. Even self-effacing Frank Kaquitts isn't above a dramatic gesture as he punctures Newman's reputation as a sure shot by disclosing that Newman uses a scatter gun instead of single bullets in his target practice.

Altman's "show" relates to another branch of the arts, painting, which he constantly refers to when talking about his movies. "I look at a film as closer to a painting or a piece of music, it's an impression," says Altman, or, reiterating an idea he frequently expresses, "The problem is, I have nothing to say, nothing to preach. It's just painting what I see," and, "I'll equate it with painting, an impression of character and total atmosphere that I am in. What happens because of what."

Altman's films are all shot in Panavision, which has an aspect ratio shaped like a rectangular painting, and this increases the force of his analogy. The complete control he exercises over the look of his films, as a painter does over his canvases, is another facet of Altman's preoccupation with painting. He talks about the appearance of *McCabe and Mrs. Miller*, gotten "from photographs. We tried to get a certain kind of antiquity look to it that would be sort of reminiscent. We could control the color. We prefogged the film to get just a little antique effect to it." Speaking of *California Split*, Altman recalls the fluorescent lighting of the scene: "That was in that first poker parlor that we used, and that's what they had out there. [Paul Lohmann, the cameraman, said,] 'This is going to look ugly on the screen, but that's the way it looks. Is that the way you want it?' I'd say, 'Sure.' We wanted that bluish cast because that's the way those Gardena Poker places look. But we didn't do the whole picture that way." Altman talks about the way he made *3 Women* look: "We overexposed all the exterior shots by three stops and printed them down, and we underexposed all the interior shots and printed them up. And we also had great color control as far as the wardrobe—Shelley Duvall's yellow dresses and Sissy Spacek's pink ones—and we painted the buildings."

All of *Nashville* is a canvas; it was part of Altman's filmic conception that most of the time the screen would be crammed with action and people, giving the impression of a postcard overflowing its borders. *Buffalo Bill* follows the same visual scheme, with its panoply of interrelated events, its swirling movements, all taking place within either the arena or the surrounding tent village.

Just as Altman's films cover the screen from corner to corner, the sound he employs fills the ear as natural, everyday sound does. Although *California Split* is the first film that officially lists "Lions Gate 8-Track Sound" as the system in which the sound was recorded, Altman had been working toward overlapping sound ever since *M*A*S*H*. That film, with its spontaneous, "impure," sometimes jumbled sound was a clear indication of the direction he wanted to go in, and *McCabe* was the second. Michael Murphy talks about how this came about: "On *McCabe* he had access to his own studio up there in Canada, so he was able to really experiment. There were no other pictures shooting in Canada, so he had access to really just play around. And to a lot of equipment. That picture works very well in a well-equipped theater. I think you hear what you need to hear. I like that sort of natural

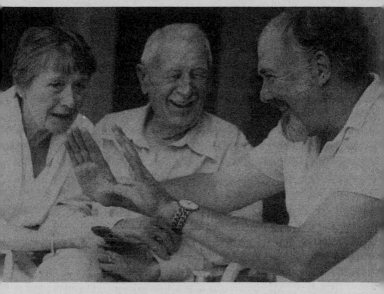

Altman chats with Ruth Nelson and longtime director John Cromwell, who appear in 3 WOMEN

feeling about it. Now he's got a thing where what he does, he records on a lot of different tracks, then he can unmix it and mix it and lay in what he wants to lay in."

Altman addresses the question of what he's trying to achieve: "Sound is supposed to be heard, but words are not necessarily supposed to be heard. I think in film it's what the character does not say, what you don't hear that is important. In [*Nashville*] we're using the eight-track sound system, and in the theaters we're adding sixteen tracks. But we're really going after the simplicity of having the audience hear what they would hear. There's no way to do that with one microphone, or with one guy mixing it there on the set, so we're getting it separated so we can get the quality we got on *California Split*. We hope this picture will be much better, because that was the first time we'd tried this system. I use earphones on the set when I'm shooting, because I want to know, not if I hear a line or whether it was delivered properly, but whether or not I got enough of a line to let me know what they're talking about. I can only do that on three of the tracks, so when I get to editing I have a lot of pleasant surprises."

In another context Altman expanded on the way he works with sound: "We have a portable eight-track sound system. It's the only one that I know of. We literally unmix our sound so that we're coming in on seven channels. On *Nashville* we augmented that with a portable sixteen-channel for the music. So we have film when the scene comes in, and we have a microphone on you and one on you and one on you back there, then we'll have one generally on the room and then there'll be one here, and all those are going into different channels so that later you can play this scene all at once. When we finish, we've got all this atmosphere to go in, and we have no dead sound effects. We have the door actually opening and we have the telephone ringing. We rig so that when we use a telephone conversation with actors, there's somebody on the other end of the line. Both are being picked up, both are being bussed to go either way, and the actor is talking to a real person on the telephone. It's unmixed. It all goes into separated channels so that when we finally cut it, we have some control. We don't have to go in and make a lot of sound effects. There's more life to it."

Whatever Altman's methodology may be, his constant tinkering and experimentation with the sound in his films has resulted in sound tracks that have a remarkably lifelike quality, a quality that results in the overall verisimilitude that he has been constantly striving toward from one film to the next. Altman's efforts all go in one direction—toward natural cinema. As he says, "I try to allow each individual to actually see and experience a different film. The attempt is to enlist an audience emotionally, not intellectually. I don't want anybody to come out with the right answer, 'cause I don't think there's any right answer. To me the perfect film would be, the people walk out of the cinema and just say, 'Wow! That was really moving,' and cannot express anything more about it, can't give it a line. In other words, it's an emotional experience, whether it's laughter or tears or . . . 'cause all these things do is trigger responses. What I want to do is get to the point where I think an audience can see a film, finish it, have an emotional response to it, and say nothing about it, not be able to articulate."

Altman tells the story about himself of a student asking him what his films were about. When Altman couldn't respond, another student supplied the answer, telling him, "Your films are about insanity." Altman agreed with this opinion. Most of Altman's films have had at least one individual who was "insane" or at least obsessed, from the Robert Duvall character in *Countdown*, who's determined to be the first man on the moon, to the person Sissy Spacek plays in *3 Women*, who inhabits another character. Overtly, no one in *McCabe and Mrs. Miller* is crazy, but the punk gunman, played by Manfred Shulz, comes close in his implacable insistence on killing Keith Carradine for no good reason.

Sandy Dennis in *That Cold Day in the Park* is literally demented, as is Robert Duvall, with his messianic religious hypocrisy, in *M*A*S*H*. "Brewster McCloud" will do anything to fly, and the lecturer in the film of that name becomes a bird. In *Images* Susannah York conjures up, and kills, figments of her imagination, and in *The Long Goodbye* Mark Rydell offers fantastic justifications for breaking a Coke bottle in his mistress's face. The same film presents Sterling Hayden as a blocked writer addled by guilt and booze, and *California Split* shows a manic

Elliott Gould and a depressive George Segal as two halves of the same obsessional gambler. *Nashville*'s Ronee Blakley suffers a breakdown while singing, and "Buffalo Bill" can't tell reality from illusion or truth from lies. The litany of fragmented personalities is likely to continue in *A Wedding*, Altman's next film.

The insanity Altman shows on screen is a social madness; it isn't a private, locked-up-in-a-booby-hatch craziness (with the exception of the Robert Duvall character in *M*A*S*H*). His films relate most directly to the screwball comedies and social justice dramas of the thirties. But madness in the seventies isn't the fey, charming whimsy it was in the thirties. The insanity Altman depicts is sour, deliberate, and streaked with sadism. *California Split* shows Gould and George Segal breaking up Bert Remsen's evening with Ann Prentiss and Gwen Welles just because they want company. They're like spoiled, asocial children who go into the sulks if they don't get their way. Gould and Donald Sutherland get Duvall tossed out of their tent in *M* A* S* H* because they don't like his fanaticism, and Sterling Hayden doesn't know whether or not he beat his mistress to a bloody pulp in *The Long Goodbye*. Altman takes the form of other movies and bends it into a quirky, mad version of itself to suit the sensibility of the seventies.

Along with the idea of social madness goes the concept of loners with visions, as Bud Cort is in *Brewster McCloud* and Warren Beatty is in *McCabe and Mrs. Miller*. These are men, or boys, stopped at some point in their adolescent development when they still believe that all things are possible. Particularly in the case of Cort, nothing can stand in his way, no act is unthinkable if it furthers his single-minded fervor. Shelley Duvall in *3*

Women is certainly alone, if unwillingly, and she conceives of herself as popular, refusing to acknowledge the fact that she's the butt of much unkind humor among her neighbors. George Segal's vision of himself in *California Split* is as a big winner. What he doesn't know is that winning destroys the dream. The only way to be a winner is never to succeed.

The worlds depicted in Altman's films are aberrant, self-enclosed microcosms. They look all right from the outside, but they're crazy when you get up close. The milieu shown in *M*A*S*H* is one in which practical jokes, anarchic black humor, and an all-pervasive denial of the real world are prevalent. *Buffalo Bill* exposes the solopsistic lack of contact with reality that prevails when men have a vested interest in maintaining someone whose grasp on truth is tenuous at best. The entire film takes place within Bill's enclave at Fort Ruth. Segal and Elliott Gould in *California Split* never see the light of day; they live their whole lives in the sickly light of poker parlors, racetracks, and prizefight arenas. They know only each other, similarly afflicted men, and a couple of hookers. *Images* shows Susannah York a prisoner of her own distorted imagination and her obsession with the book she's writing about elves and unicorns. Shelley Duvall journeys back and forth, in *3 Women*, between her home and the spa where she works, with regular side trips to look for men in the bar at Dodge City. "Brewster McCloud" has virtually imprisoned himself beneath the Houston Astrodome while working on his wings, and Sandy Dennis literally imprisons young Michael Burns, in *That Cold Day in the Park*. Even as far back as *Countdown*, which has no thematic connection with the rest of Altman's work, the astronauts know nothing but their work, to the exclusion of all but the most minimal relations with their families.

In *Thieves Like Us*, the protagonists have trapped themselves in a tiny world which includes only the banks they rob, Tom Skerritt's gas-station hideout, and whatever home Louise Fletcher is making for them at the moment. And *A Wedding*, which Altman started filming in June of 1977, takes place entirely during one day and encompasses a wedding and the reception which follows it.

Altman likes to take a particular genre and break the form. He made *M*A*S*H* as an antiwar comedy that was so chaotic, so deliberately anarchic, that he seems to have said everything worth saying about the futility of war. *McCabe and Mrs. Miller* had a hooker for a heroine and a not-very-bright failed entrepreneur for a hero; it was a western only in that there was a shootout between the bad guys and the hero at the end. *The Long Goodbye* presented the quintessential detective, Philip Marlowe, as hip, sloppy, and cool. *Nashville* told America that our politicians were fools and our folk heroes sex-mad and success-crazy, hardly a burning revelation after the antics of Watergate. But it was the *form* that *Nashville* took that was the revelation; it was a kaleidescope of impressions, vignettes, and thumbnail portraits. The minute the viewer started concentrating on what a character was doing or saying, or where his actions were leading, Altman cut away to another set of characters. He kept firm control of the film, though; *Nashville* may be impressionistic in style, but its realization is concrete. *Buffalo Bill* takes the Western success story and turns it upside down.

The structure of any Altman film is deliberately unsettling. Altman takes parallel editing to the point of

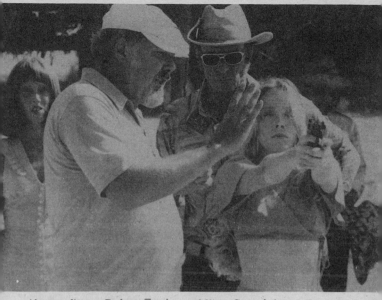

Altman directs Robert Fortier and Sissy Spacek in a scene for 3 WOMEN as Shelley Duvall looks on

fracturing his film. This is particularly noticeable in *Buffalo Bill*, with its constant jumps between Bill's activities and Ned Buntline's carping commentary, delivered from the bar, but it was foreshadowed in *M*A*S*H*, which used the operating room as a sort of splicing device to separate the various events but keep them firmly held together, as a form of thematic bridge. *Images* also used a connective motif, the tinkling wind chimes, to blend the disjointed and disturbing actions into a whole. In *Nashville* Altman has a large group of characters to cut among. As he says, "I have twenty-four people going, and if I get bored with what one person is saying, I'll just cut over to somebody else and come back and pick him up later." The result is a fragmented but ultimately cohesive film, which makes a definite political and social statement. In *Thieves Like Us*, although the film is cut more or less conventionally, using parallel editing to make the transitions between the activities of Keechie and Bowie and Chicamaw and T-Dub, Altman also uses the 1930s radio programs as a connecting theme, and as a comment on the events that were taking place on the screen. For example, President Roosevelt's voice is heard talking about prosperity as the three robbers demonstrate the lengths they're forced to go to (by choice, as much as by Depression-inspired necessity) by stealing from a bank.

Like the bank robbers in *Thieves*, most Altman protagonists are hopeful in the face of odds that to an ordinary citizen would signify impending disaster. The three men in this film ignore the fact that the law, which has seen fit to print their pictures and offer rewards in a detective magazine, is obviously closing in on them (although it is, in fact, Louise Fletcher who contacts the "laws" and turns Keith Carradine in). Warren Beatty in *McCabe*, although concerned enough to see a lawyer, pretends to himself that the mining company that wants to buy his holdings doesn't care enough to have him killed. Each character in an Altman film comforts himself by refusing to see the truth around him and nourishes himself with ideas of his own invincibility and ability to overcome whatever obstacles are placed in his path. Elliott Gould and Donald Sutherland in *M*A*S*H* simply batter their way through any hurdles that get in their way, either physically or with their own brand of idiotic humor. "Brewster McCloud" permits no hindrance, emotional, monetary or material, to interfere with his vision of flying in the Astrodome. Gould, in *The*

Long Goodbye, insists on knowing the truth of his friend's death despite the lack of cooperation he gets from the police and from his own client. The heroes of *California Split* make a quest of the big win at gambling when any moderately astute student of psychology could tell them that not only are they undercapitalized, but the real high comes from playing, not from winning, and they're courting a big letdown by going for big stakes in Reno. Gwen Welles ignores the fact of her own lack of talent in *Nashville*, as Geraldine Chaplin ignores the obvious—that most people find her an obnoxious nitwit. Barbara Harris is oblivious of the concept that, try as she will, she has very little hope of making it in big-time country-and-western music. "Buffalo Bill" pretends that he can outwit and outmaneuver Frank Kaquitts, although it's clear that any confrontation between them is bound to end in a stalemate, and Geraldine Chaplin ignores the fact of her own fallibility, pretending, when she misses a target, that she hasn't, and taking the shot over again. Shelley Duvall of *3 Women* refuses to acknowledge the fact that she isn't popular, either with her co-workers at the spa or with the young singles at her apartment, although she does, when forced to, become a more responsible individual, assuming the care first of her roommate, Sissy Spacek, and later of Janice Rule.

Along with this idea of flying in the face of what would normally be considered the accepted wisdom is the notion that Altman's characters are, for the most part, hapless gamblers or romantic, foolish visionaries. To some degree, so is Altman himself, although his movies are, on the surface, cool and distant, with a sense of being rueful observations, rather than committed polemics. Such are the doctors played by Gould and Sutherland in

M*A*S*H who gamble that they can keep madness at bay with their sophomoric pranks and black humor. *Brewster McCloud* is the most quixotic dreamer of all Altman's heroes, with his insistence on scaling the Astrodome's heights, gambling that he can do it without falling and that his luck will hold out. *McCabe's* is a more practical vision, with his notion of fiscal gain via whores and gambling in the Northwest and his personal gamble that he and Mrs. Miller can bring it off and hold their own against the mining company that wants to buy him out. Susannah York's *Images* are visions of dead lovers, returned to haunt her, and Elliott Gould, in *The Long Goodbye*, takes a chance that he can discover the truth of his friend's death; his folly is that the people with whom he is involved aren't as interested in truth and justice as he is. Although the robbers of *Thieves Like Us* don't really believe they can go on forever, they behave as though they can; they have a romantic concept of themselves as entrepreneurs, and they senselessly gamble with their lives and their futures. *California Split* literally is about gambling, and its putative heroes naïvely deny the real world, preferring to behave like overgrown adolescents, selfishly following their own desires and ignoring the wishes of others or the responsibilities owed to the world around them. Gwen Welles and Barbara Harris of *Nashville* both have delusions about their abilities to become country-and-western stars, and both gamble that they can. Ronee Blakley gambles with her health and her sanity to please her public and her husband; Michael Murphy gambles with his political future that he can bring off the rally for his candidate. "Buffalo Bill" isn't the only absurd visionary—so are his sycophantic aides, Joel Grey and Kevin McCarthy, who nourish his megalomania and massage his ego, gambling that they can hold him together long enough to make a fortune from his legend. In *3 Women* Shelley Duvall's foolish romanticism stems from her conception of herself as a popular, with-it young lady and negates the truth of her position—she is an object of scorn to those with whom she most wishes to consort.

But the most romantic gambler of all is Altman, who literally risks his money wagering for big stakes, and his reputation and future gambling that the public, and to a lesser degree the critics, who usually take to his films, will accept what he's trying on the screen. As Altman says: "To be a gambler, the risk has to be devastating. If you're a gambler, what you have to lose is your total security. Money represents security . . . and there's a certain *joie de vivre* when you get close to danger, your body sets up for it . . . but for a gambler that's dangerous, because the risks have to keep escalating. If I win or lose ten thousand dollars in a poker game, and next time I'm playing in a game, top two hundred dollars, it's no fun. . . . I have good years and bad years. Year before last, I won about twenty-six thousand dollars; but I never stop while I'm winning. I may bet five hundred or a thousand dollars on a game, but you always lose in the long run because of the percentages." When asked specifically if there's a connection between his gambling instincts and his career, Altman replies, "Only in the sense that if you've experienced life as a gambler, you realize you can get along without great security. Consequently, it doesn't bother me when there's no money in the bank. I have this optimistic attitude that nobody's going to starve."

If Altman gambles in making his films, he also takes a huge risk when he turns them over to the distributor to release and promote. Historically, his distributors have shown less understanding of how his films should be sold than his audiences and critics have of what he's trying to say in each film. As Altman remarks, "The studio advertising people, for the most part, have no idea what the film is 'about,' and their ad campaigns lure people in and then these people don't see what they expected to see. I try to exercise some control in the advertising campaign. I didn't have any on *California Split*. I was told I did, but I didn't. If I got into the selling business, I wouldn't have time to make pictures. So I try to do the best I can. Those guys who sell films don't like movies, really. They're still in the carnival business, where it's 'Get their quarter, get them in the tent, and get out quick.' The first ads of *The Long Goodbye* were Elliott Gould with a gun and a cigarette dangling from his lips. Then they tried to clean him up and make him look like Humphrey Bogart. It's misleading. The audience that may like to see that film and would respond to it will look at that ad and they'll stay away from the theater, and the people who go to see the other kind of film will hate the picture. So it's a flop. But I can't say exactly what the campaign should be. When we released it in New York with the *Mad* magazine campaign, that was my campaign. That worked very, very successfully in New York, but they had already dissipated most of the major markets with this other thing and it was already a flop. On *Nashville*, now, already [speaking in 1975] we have artwork done, and I have this advantage because though it's going to be a Paramount release, it's ABC's investment. We've already done a lot of that stuff, and when we come and hand them this material, they're going to be more prone to taking it, I think." Late in 1976

Altman had the following exchange with an interviewer on the same subject:

> INTERVIEWER: To my way of thinking, *Buffalo Bill* was horribly marketed. Did you have anything to do with the marketing end of it?
>
> ALTMAN: I did—with the ads.
>
> INTERVIEWER: For instance, that "Sitting Bull Says Bull"?
>
> ALTMAN: That was my idea.
>
> INTERVIEWER: It didn't work, did it?
>
> ALTMAN: I guess not. The idea was to try to let people know what the tone of the picture was.
>
> INTERVIEWER: The tone really isn't "Sitting Bull Says Bull," like the ads say, is it?
>
> ALTMAN: I wanted the idea that it was something to make you laugh at, and that Buffalo Bill was full of shit.

Such have been Altman's negative experiences with studios and the distribution of his films that after United Artists had begun press screenings of *Welcome to L.A.*, he withdrew the film. The distributor circulated a press release that said in part: "United Artists and producer Robert Altman have entered into an agreement whereby the theatrical distribution rights to *Welcome to L.A.* will revert to Altman's Lion's Gate Films for a period of three years.... Altman commended United Artists for its all-out sales, advertising and promotional support to date. 'They used our marketing approach and permitted one of my associates, Mike Kaplan, to personally supervise each of the openings. UA has been generous and supportive throughout,' Altman said."

In 1976, after *Buffalo Bill* failed at the box office, Dino De Laurentiis kicked Altman off the projected movie version of E. L. Doctorow's *Ragtime*, and Altman voluntarily withdrew from Warner Brothers' *The Yig Epoxy*, a film which was to star Peter Falk in a script by Altman and Alan Rudolph. Falk later sued Warner Brothers to collect some of the money he was owed contractually. Altman was further frustrated by being unable to obtain the rights to Kurt Vonnegut, Jr.'s *Breakfast of Champions*, a project which is still up in the air. As he says, referring to whether or not he'll ever be able to make the film: "I don't know what's going to happen. If I can cast it and get that college student that bought it to stop trying to milk us for money every day. Now he's refused to sign the contract. I have a great script, I mean a really good script, for *Breakfast of Champions*. It's all cast except the leading role, and we're just having problems with an... arrogance."

Robert Altman went back to Twentieth Century-Fox, for the first time since *M* A* S* H*, to do *3 Women*. As he states, "It's a very comfortable place right now," and so his next project, *A Wedding*, which began shooting in June of 1977, is being made for Fox.

And so Altman continues to consolidate and enlarge upon his growing popularity as a filmmaker by playing variations upon his greatest virtues: his startling originality, the fact that he never makes the same film twice, and his consistent use of "American" themes. Even *Images*, which is the only motion picture he has made abroad, has as its text the mental and emotional disintegration of an individual, a subject which has intrigued American filmmakers as diverse as Mitchell Leisen (*Lady in the Dark*), Robert Siodmak (*The Dark Mirror*), and

Nunnally Johnson (*The Three Faces of Eve*). *M* A* S* H*
concerns an American war and the efforts of a group of
medics to stave off boredom and encroaching insanity
with a peculiarly American brand of humor. *Brewster
McCloud* is a perverted version of the American success
story, dealing with accomplishment and expediency, two
qualities that anyone who is familiar with the history of
the Watergate episode in American politics knows is a
common facet of our way of life. *McCabe and Mrs. Miller*
and *Buffalo Bill* deal with the American dream gone
awry, the former through stupidity and lack of vision, the
latter through feeding a myth that has only itself and its
own lies to believe in. *California Split* is another variation
on the sourness of success, the achievement that palls as
soon as it's been accomplished. As Oscar Wilde noted, "In
this world there are only two tragedies. One is not getting
what one wants, and the other is getting it." The detective
genre, although heartily embraced by the French, is a
peculiarly American phenomenon, one which Altman
was able to wring some variations on, in the course of
making his naïve/sour rendition of *The Long Goodbye*.
Thieves Like Us is an anti-celebration of American
entrepreneurship which, instead of presenting its protagonists as canny, if crooked, capitalists, in the manner of
many of its predecessors, depicted them as ignorant rubes
doomed to failure. *Nashville*, with its focus on country-
and-western music and politics, is in a typically American
milieu, where success means being current and failure is
signified by being out of touch with the mainstream, or,
more disastrously, with oneself.

In spite of the frequently bitter viewpoint he takes in
approaching each film, Altman is an optimist. He *hopes*
for something better, but, being a realist, he presents his

version of the truth, a slightly negative, determinedly ironic, highly idiosyncratic and deeply personal vision of America, a place Altman obviously loves, but which he shows with all its warts left on. He clearly loves making films, and he wants everyone to come to his party.

As Robert Altman tells it: "I want each one of my pictures to be different. Then [after my next film] it will be something else... but it will be what I want... and it will be done the way I think it should be done.

"There is a special concern a director must have. It's a sort of love thing between him, the people on the set, and the property they are doing. I want my pictures to be a part of me, and I want to be a part of my pictures. It has to be a twenty-four-hour-a-day love thing.

"I think it is important to want to go one step further. I find great satisfaction in directing. Sure, there are great limitations placed on me today—but perhaps tomorrow it will all be different."

The Delinquents

"*Well, this guy back there* [in Kansas City] *said he had the money to make a picture, if I'd make it about delinquents. I said okay, and I wrote the thing in five days, cast it, picked the locations, drove the generator truck, got the people together, took no money, and we just did it, that's all. My motives at that time were to make a picture, and if they'd said I gotta shoot it in green in order to get it done, I'd say, 'Well, I can figure a way to do that.' I would have done anything to get the thing done.*"

Today, although Altman owns a print, he is not anxious to share his first film with the public. While he maintains he is not embarrassed about his directorial debut, Altman says, "Nobody knew what they were doing. I don't think it has any meaning to anybody."

The Delinquents is the sort of consummately silly movie many directors turn out as a first film. Altman was no François Truffaut, and he didn't have Paris to use as a background the way Truffaut did for *The 400 Blows*. Altman was stuck with suburban Kansas City.

The Delinquents features a great many raw, underlit interiors, overexposed exterior shots, and erratically moving shadows. It looks the way John Cassavetes's first movie, *Shadows*, would have looked had it been made out

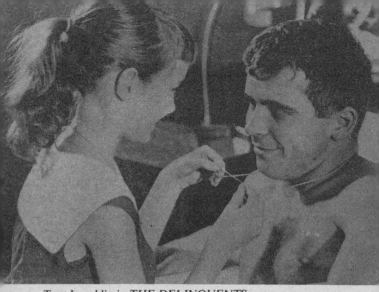

Tom Laughlin in THE DELINQUENTS

of doors. But it tells the same story *Rebel Without a Cause* told two years earlier. It even uses some locations of the same kind: a police station and an abandoned mansion.

The story concerns Scotty (Tom Laughlin), a young man in love with Janice (Rosemary Howard), whose father doesn't want her going steady at the tender age of sixteen. Scotty's mother nags about his using the car too much, while his father sympathizes with his plight and gives him the car keys anyway. Scotty runs into Cholly (Peter Miller) and his gang at a drive-in, and Cholly, posing as a good guy, offers to date Janice and bring her to Scotty. (This device is still being used eighteen years later, notably by Lisa Alther in *Kinflicks*.) *The Delinquents'* one effective and well-played scene shows Cholly snowing Janice's parents with a line about working in the stock market and wanting to get ahead. A party at the mansion ends with a police raid, and Scotty is blamed for calling the cops. The gang kidnaps Janice in revenge, and

Scotty rescues her and beats Cholly to a pulp.

The film features a redundant and pointless narration, spoken in tones of darkest foreboding, about the "teenage violence and immaturity" that saps "the moral fiber of our great nation." At the end (the voice is used as if in preachy parentheses) the narrator asks "who's to blame?" for this "crippling disease," and suggests that "church groups" should step in to counsel troubled adolescents and their parents. Contemporary audiences hoot at this narration, at the hairstyles (duck's-ass cuts for the boys, page-boys for the girls) and at the clothes (chinos, penny loafers, and crinolines); swoon over the cars, and howl with sarcastic glee at the social attitudes. Kissing and petting are a big deal; going steady (a now archaic term) is tantamount to being engaged, and nobody "does it." The results of all this repressed sexuality, on the evidence of *The Delinquents*, are slashed tires, teenage hangovers, and the hassles one's parents dish out for irresponsible behavior. In fact, *The Delinquents* indicts uncaring, overzealous disciplinarian adults as severely as *Rebel Without a Cause* does, but without the careful motivation the Nicholas Ray/Stewart Stern script develops to explain the outbursts of hoodlumism in that film. One would like to absolve Altman of blame for the use of a poorly written narration for his film, but he and Stern are guilty of using (and overusing) the same device in *The James Dean Story*.

Two performances stand out: Peter Miller's Cholly, a slimy, mock-sincere charmer, and Richard Bakalyn's psychotic, jived-up Eddy. As Altman reported, Laughlin is a poor carbon copy of James Dean, mannered and self-conscious, but he nevertheless intimates that, given a better vehicle, he could develop into a promising actor. Rosemary Howard is gauche and unconvincing, but the child who plays Scotty's young sister, Sissy (Christine Altman, the director's daughter), has a natural and unaffected presence.

Altman remembers that Laughlin (later famous for his *Billy Jack* movies) "was just an unbelievable pain in the ass. Total egomaniac. He was so angry he wasn't a priest. Big Catholic hangup. This Laughlin kid was doing all the things he'd heard about James Dean doing."

The trade papers found *The Delinquents* gory and sensational, but praised the technical acumen with which the film was made.

The James Dean Story

The James Dean Story was an unsuccessful attempt to capitalize on the dead movie star's short-lived screen popularity. It's a rather ordinary compilation film that seeks to add luster to a tradition of dubious film documentaries—the psychobiography. Although George W. George and Altman, who coproduced and codirected the film, and Stewart Stern, who wrote it, undoubtedly felt they had some insights into the emotional makeup of both Dean and the teen-agers who either worshipped or emulated him, apparently they were insufficient to guarantee the film success at the box office. The film failed both critically and commercially and was quickly sold to television. Marlon Brando was asked to narrate and gave serious consideration to the idea: "Toward the end I think he was beginning to find his own way as an actor. But this glorifying of Dean is all wrong. That's why I believe the documentary could be important. To show he wasn't a hero; show what he really was—just a lost boy trying to find himself." But Brando eventually refused, and Martin Gabel took on the assignment. He reads Stern's ponderous phrases like a guide in a mortuary. There is no hint, in either the narration or the style in which it was read, that the creators of the film understood what Dean was all about—that he was, as Brando put it,

43

"a lost boy trying to find himself" and doing a bad job of it. Altman and George have turned up some interesting footage—a screen test for *East of Eden* and a highway-safety film Dean made with Gig Young.

Since the film was released by Warner Brothers, the studio that had produced all of Dean's films, it's surprising that the only commercial footage of him on the screen, besides the safety short and the test with Richard Davalos, is from *Rebel Without a Cause*. It would have been far more effective to use his tormented screen persona than the shots of a dead seagull washing around in the Pacific, which Stern's narration likens to Dean's unfulfilled dreams. The effect of this kind of silliness is to obscure Dean rather than expose him. The most effective scenes are those among the people in New York who knew him before he made a hit on the stage in André Gide's *The Immoralist* and left for California. There's a moon-eyed young lady, Arleen Langer, who was in love with him and who kept some of his things when he departed, and the bartender and owner of a spaghetti joint on Fifty-second Street where Dean mooched meals and played his bongo drums. These two jovially sinister gentlemen had a real appreciation for Dean's idiosyncrasies and refuse to allow the inquiring documentarians to draw them into any overanalysis of Dean's foibles.

A few of his fraternity brothers at UCLA speculate on what he might have been like if he'd stayed long enough for them to know him, as does a young writer who knew him in California. Most of the people who had really known Dean refused to have anything to do with the film, people such as Nicholas Ray, Elia Kazan, who directed his first two films, and Pier Angeli with whom he was reportedly in love and who is alluded to ambiguously by showing her name on a movie marquee.

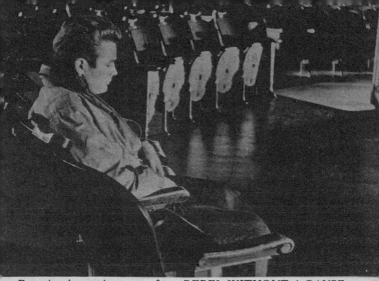

Dean in planetarium scene from REBEL WITHOUT A CAUSE.

By far the most irritating technique Altman and George employed was that of a "distant figure," an individual of Dean's size and build who is used as a stand-in, in locations from Dean's youth in Fairmount, Indiana. Fairmount is the only place where the filmmakers found cooperative subjects for their prying cameras. Dean's aunt and uncle, with whom he lived, talk with affection for "Jimmy" and show the camera snapshots of Dean as a boy. The man who sold Dean his first motorcycle, his teacher (to whom he gave one of his paintings), and many others are pressed into service to explain the "riddle" of James Dean. In spite of all these reminiscences, Altman and George repeatedly cut back to this "distant figure," gamboling with a dog or walking near a pond in a frozen landscape. Not content with this device, Altman and George engage in what the preface to the film calls "the dynamic exploration of the still photo"—in other words they pan across snapshots, portraits, news photos, anything they think will yield up the "secret" of this mysterious and haunted young man.

And Stern's narration piles it on with a trowel: Dean possessed "the lonely awareness that growing up is pain," his death meant that "youth mourned itself in the passing of James Dean," and the commentary seeks to explain his passion for motorcycles by claiming that "to test the limits of life he had to approach the borders of death."

There are bits of truth in all this pseudopsychological attitudinizing, but it's hard to sort them out from all the blinding insights that occurred after Dean's death. The film is much better as a portrait of an era—the fifties. Dean belongs to that "silent generation" of "beatniks" who felt nothing but apathy at the Korean War or Joseph McCarthy's anti-Communist hysteria. In the grubby New York of the mid-fifties, when all girls looked like Audrey Hepburn and all boys like Tony Curtis, there was nothing special about the young man who was born James Byron in 1931. What was special was the way those young Hepburns and Curtises worshipped Dean and made him into something he never could have been—an ageless idol, the representation of their youth and the repository of their fantasies.

Countdown

It's almost impossible to see any way in which *Countdown* is a Robert Altman film. It was made as a programmer in 1968, and Altman was fired before he could cut the film because he wanted to have more than one actor talking on the sound track at the same time. Costar Michael Murphy recalls that *Countdown* was just one of a series of low-budget films being produced at that time: "They were a million dollars or less, and all that was expected of that unit at Warner Brothers was co-features, so they didn't want anything very special, and they, by God, weren't going to have anything very special. He directed the picture, then they took it away from him and gave it to an editor, and they put in a lot of loops. The producer went out and reshot the ending. It was a real disaster. They cut Bob right out of the picture."

The story line is a preface to the moon shot that took place the following year, in July. It's a "might have happened this way" story, the kind that looks just slightly better than a TV movie when seen on television. NASA executive Ross (Steve Ihnat) tells Lee (James Caan), Rick (Michael Murphy), and Chiz (Robert Duvall) to halt their preparations for the moon shot because the President has decided that the U.S. astronaut should be a civilian. Chiz, who was the original choice, is bitter at losing his chance, but agrees to train Lee. Lee lands on the moon and finds the Russians already there, but dead. He spots the shelter beacon blinking, and the film ends as he walks to the shelter where he will spend the next year until the more up-to-date Apollo can arrive to take him back to Earth.

The real star of *Countdown* is the art director, Jack Poplin, who designed extraordinarily faithful duplicates of the space modules used in the real-life moon shot the following summer. There's a nod in the direction of a conventional romantic story with Joanna Moore as Mickey, Lee's wife, and Barbara Baxley as Chiz's wife, Jean, accompanying their respective husbands everywhere and looking worried or drinking too much,

Steve Ihnat, James Caan, and Robert Duvall in COUNT-DOWN

James Caan

Ihnat, Caan, and Duvall with some of the film's impressive hardware

The Russian capsule on the moon

but Altman didn't put any stress on this aspect, nor did Loring Mandel's screenplay. The performances are conventional and sturdy; the best are Steve Ihnat's and Robert Duvall's. Duvall's role, probably by coincidence, is a forecast of the kind of part he would do a year later in *M*A*S*H*. The film is so tightly scripted that improvisation would not only be improbable but impossible, so that the supercontrolled surface beginning to crack that Duvall does so well has no chance to emerge from the confines of Altman's tightly supervised camerawork. The only hint of personal idiosyncrasy, so dear to the heart of the Altman rough diamond, is evidenced by Bobby Riha, Jr., who plays Lee's son, Stevie, with a pet rubber mouse hanging from his neck.

The *New York Times* reviewer crucified the film, saying: "We'll never believe those fellows ran out of oxygen. They were bored to death."

Altman describes how he came to make *Countdown* and what happened when the film was completed: "*Countdown* was based on a book I'd tried to option for myself, Hank Searls's *The Pilgrim Project*, and I had a yen to do it. I think we made a good little picture out of it—except for the editing, which was Jack Warner's idea. With just a few days [of shooting] left, the old man asked to see an assemblage. 'Jesus Christ!' he said. 'You've got all the actors talking at once! Who's going to understand it?' What Warner did was to cut the picture for kids. Which is the reverse of what I was going for. In theory, the film was about a moon shot; but what interested me was the human situation behind such endeavors: the petty politics, the bitchiness of the wives, that sort of thing. The cut Warner did played the obvious. It became a lot of flag waving."

That Cold Day in the Park

That Cold Day in the Park can't make up its mind what it wants to be—a stylish horror film, a compassionate study of spinsterhood a la Brian Moore's *The Lonely Passion of Judith Hearne*, or a study of postadolescent drop-outs living in Canada. It's a thoroughly plotted, conventionally scripted story of a young woman who lives in Vancouver, B.C., and one rainy day spots a young man huddled on a park bench. Sandy Dennis as Frances Austen, lonely, wealthy, and aimless, invites the boy (Michael Burns) in to dry off. She feeds him, puts him to sleep in her guest room, and buys him clothes the next day. The boy expresses his gratitude by dancing, clad in a towel, to some Middle Eastern music. He slips out to get some money from his family and to see his sister, who gives him some marijuana brownies to take back with him. The boy has given Frances the impression that he's mute, but this is revealed as a game he plays to put people on. Frances gets high on the drugged cookies and plays blindman's buff, using her old school tie as the blindfold. In the middle of the game the boy slips away. Frances talks constantly, her chatter filling in the gaps that the boy refuses to supply; it masks the fact that she's becoming attracted to him. She's fitted for a contraceptive device in anticipation of seducing the boy, but he goes out again, in

Sandy Dennis in THAT COLD DAY IN THE PARK

spite of the fact that she locks him in his room at night. His sister Nina (Suzanne Benton) visits him and taunts him with incestuous overtures. Frances finds a prostitute, whom she brings home for him and murders with a knife while the boy is making love to her. Having nailed the windows shut, Frances babbles about how she can't let him go and makes it clear that, however fond of him she may be, he's her prisoner.

That Cold Day in the Park presages *Images* in its use of mirrors and glass as devices that signal a mind disintegrating. Altman also uses the sound of a music box, which is echoed by the wind chimes in the later film and foreshadows the use of the same instrument in *McCabe and Mrs. Miller*. Sandy Dennis is playing the same sort of repressed spinster she did in *The Fox*, with the same facial tics she used in *Who's Afraid of Virginia Woolf?* Fortunately she's less mannered here, so Frances Austen, for all her unexplained motivation, is a more sympathetic character. The problem with Frances is that she's neither desperate enough nor crazy enough to fully enlist an audience's sympathy. It isn't sufficient to have her proposed to by a doctor she finds repellent, or to be surrounded by middle-aged servants and relatives, or to lead a rich, idle life. She has to be a figure one can identify with on some level; there must be a reason for her behavior, and the script (by Gillian Freeman) supplies none. The audience must believe she is *going* mad, not that she is sane one minute and crazy the next.

The scene that best delineates the process of sliding into insanity shows Frances, who has been repulsed by the boy as an object of sexual desirability, searching nighttime Vancouver for a prostitute to bring home to him. She sits alone in a bar while a friendly group at a table nearby talks and laughs. She follows a coarse-looking, overly

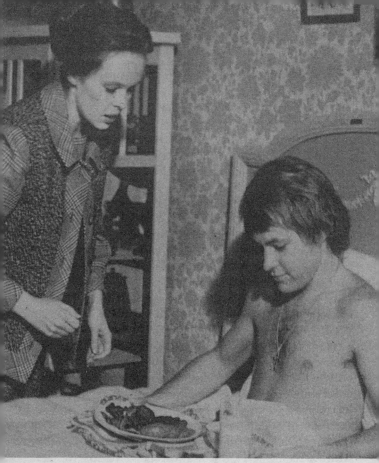

Sandy Dennis serves breakfast to Michael Burns

made-up woman into the ladies' room and propositions her for "a friend who can't go out." The whore calls Frances a pervert and storms angrily out, but a man (identified in the cast list as The Rounder and played by Michael Murphy) follows her into the street and says he can help her. The Rounder leads Frances to an all-night café where he makes a connection. A few minutes later a thin, exhausted-looking prostitute named Sylvia turns

Sandy Dennis

up, a deal is struck, and Frances takes the girl home with her.

(Murphy remembers how he came to play this part: "I was doing another picture, and I had like two weeks off and I came up to sort of hang around. Bob said, 'Well, while you're here, why don't you play this part?' And I said, 'Great!' It was an interesting idea 'cause the guy was a real heavy. So the first scene I played with [Sandy

Dennis], we're out on the street and it's cold as hell and I had to kind of catch up with her, walking behind her, going, 'Miss, Miss!' or something. She turned around and there was such contact I couldn't move. It was sexual. My heart was pounding and I'm going, 'Ohhhwwh!' It was such a high. It was a really terrific experience. It was a small film and fun to do, and weird as it was, everybody was kind of nice and fun to be around—very, very positive, as are most of his movies.")

In contrast to the formal, well-organized life Frances leads, Altman has shown the seamy, tawdry underside of Vancouver. Frances's disorientation, the fact that she has no mechanisms for dealing with these people, is very well demonstrated. She stammers and flounders, trying to use the mode of behavior that stands her in good stead at bowling competitions and tea parties, but it's no use. She's in control at home, but here she's powerless, and she gasps in confusion, her flickering eyes betraying her awkwardness and anxiety.

Frances takes the girl back with her and gives her to the boy like a present. She listens as they make love and then moves away from the door. Altman plays with the audience's expectations at this point: We think there'll be something more and are fooled when she goes away. But suddenly she leaps into the room and bounces, screaming with laughter, on the bed. It isn't until a few minutes later that the knife is discovered, plunged into Sylvia's heart. The boy cowers in the hall, trying to hide, but Frances sees him and comfortingly tells him that she told the girl to go, that it's all right, he shouldn't be frightened. Frances kisses the boy gently, soothingly, as the chimes are heard dimly in the background. Frances has made the boy her prisoner and she is politely crazy.

Lacking any real motivation for Frances's actions

beyond the not very satisfactory one that she's a thwarted spinster, Altman has filled the movie with surfaces that glitter and reflect. The film is so full of objects it looks like an industrial film or a television commercial for chrome. In noting this phenomenon, Hollis Alpert, writing in the *Saturday Review*, said: "In case we fail to notice Miss Dennis's mental imbalance, the refractions from the windows make it quite clear. Eventually, it all becomes too much. There are some scary moments, but some that are unintentionally ludicrous, too, and we get the impression that everyone has tried much too hard to make a stylish, mature, sexy horror film—aimed at today's box office."

The subsidiary members of the cast, particularly those in the movie's first scene, are very good at suggesting the kind of world Frances wants to get away from, with their fussiness and petty comments, their rich, inbred conservatism, but this is never made the cause of Frances's lapse from sanity.

David Hutchinson, who criticized *That Cold Day in the Park* for *Films and Filming*, said, "Despite the weaknesses of the script, director Robert Altman keeps one's attention from wandering; although he is unable to create the necessary sense of tension and claustrophobia to make the plot's wilder flights of fancy believable. A number of his stylistic touches, including the unnecessary use of the hand-held camera and self-conscious and labored cross-cutting in the scene of the doctor's proposal to Frances, are irritating; but he uses color intelligently to create atmosphere contrasting the pale tones of the park, Frances' apartment, and the clinic with the hot garish colors of the night exteriors, the sister's pad, and the bars where Frances searches for a prostitute."

*M * A * S * H*

If war is a metaphor for insanity, then *M*A*S*H* is a parallel for the snake pit. In the film the chaos and disrespect for human life of the battlefield is equalled and countered by the anarchy and repair of those lives in the operating room. Robert Altman's *M*A*S*H* is a film about an event of the early fifties, the Korean War, made with a late-sixties sensibility as an obvious reference to Vietnam. Late 1969 and early 1970, when *M* A* S* H* was released, was a time, still, of great dissension within the United States. *Catch-22*, *The Strawberry Statement*, and *Getting Straight*, among others, came out later that year and also sought to capitalize on the mood of national disenchantment. Twentieth Century–Fox released *Patton* the same week, and according to Michael Murphy, who plays Me Lay Marston in *M* A* S* H*, it was the coincidence in release dates which enabled *M* A* S* H* to come out in the form it did: "The people at the studio had said, 'Don't touch the negative.' [Altman] went ahead and cut it anyway. They had *Patton* going on and they were paying more attention to *Patton* than they were to Bob's picture. So he kind of slipped through. He put the picture together and we started going around to these screenings for critics. One night the whole foreign press got up and walked out of the screening because of the blood and all of that, and they were very haughty about it all. The guy in *Variety* came in with a look of great decisions about him, and he gave it a big, terrible panning and the studio, all the publicity guys said 'Ahhw, it's a piece of shit, schlep it out the back door,' and all that. Then it went to San Francisco and it happened to be a real raucous Saturday night. They were there seeing *Butch Cassidy*, and it was a big downtown theatre, packed to the rafters, and people went absolutely berserk. People were stomping on the floor and carrying on. It was the most exciting thing I've ever seen. And *that's* the reason the picture got released the way it did. And the guy from *Variety* said, 'Well, they screwed me. The studio told me...' That's where his integrity was. It just picked up momentum and it was against all odds that it took off the way it did."

M*A*S*H took off to the tune of almost forty-one million dollars total grosses, according to *Variety*. It won the Grand Prize at Cannes in 1970 and was the National Society of Film Critics' choice for best film of that year. Sally Kellerman was nominated for an Academy Award as best supporting actress and the film was nominated for best film (They lost to Helen Hayes in *Airport*, and to *Patton*, Fox's other contender, respectively). Altman was nominated for best director, but only Ring Lardner, Jr., collected an Oscar—for a script Altman took a great many liberties with. *M*A*S*H* is still regarded by many as one of the quintessential anti-war films, along with *Catch-22, All Quiet on the Western Front, Paths of Glory*, and *Dr. Strangelove*, among others.

The plot, such as it is, derives from Richard Hooker's novel and concerns three surgeons, captains assigned to the 4077th MASH (Mobile Army Surgical Hospital), three miles behind the front in Korea. They are "Hawkeye" Pierce (Donald Sutherland), "Trapper John"

Donald Sutherland as Hawkeye in M*A*S*H

McIntyre (Elliott Gould), and "Duke" Forrest (Tom Skerritt), who inhabit "the Swamp," or officer's tent, with Major Frank Burns (Robert Duvall) until Burns cracks up. Burns has a fling with Major Margaret Houlihan (Kellerman) which the entire camp hears on the public-address system and which gives the major her nickname, "Hot Lips." The Painless Pole, "the dental Don Juan of Detroit," (John Schuck) suffers a bout of impotence, diagnoses himself as a latent homosexual, and decides to commit suicide—with a little help from his friends. Instead of a lethal "black capsule," Painless gets a tranquilizer and the companionship of Lieutenant Dish, which quickly restores him to his former self. The men rig the shower to collapse so they can find out whether or not Hot Lips is a natural blonde. Trapper and Hawkeye fly to Japan to operate on a congressman's wounded son. The 325th Evac. and the 4077th MASH arrange a football game, the 4077th conspires to bring in a "ringer," "Spearchucker" Jones (Fred Williamson), and rig the game so they can up the ante. Through the use of sedatives, a semi-eligible play, and other devious tactics, the MASH unit triumphs in a last-minute victory. The film ends with the departure of Hawkeye and Duke, while business as usual, the arrival of more wounded and the exodus of recuperated soldiers, takes place at the camp.

The entire movie takes place within the time Pierce and Forrest are at the MASH company. It begins with their arrival and ends with their departure; the greatest achievement of their stay in Korea is not the number of mangled bodies they have reassembled, but that they have managed to remain sane.

In spite of being so close to the front, the war seems far away. There are no shots of doctors looking at planes above and murmuring, "I hope that's one of ours." The tangible reminders of war are the camouflaged tents, the grim muddiness, the overall khaki color of everything, and most prominently, of course, the dead, dying, and wounded casualties of the nearby "police action." The events of *M*A*S*H* are intercut with the MASH unit's operations, extremely bloody and graphic surgery performed on a never-ending stream of wounded that flows into the camp. The spirit of the film (and of the company) is captured most precisely in the operating-room scenes and in the song Pfc. Seidman (Ken Prymus) sings at Painless's near-demise, "Suicide Is Painless."

The operating-room scenes, which act as the cohering thread holding the film together, had been expanded by Ring Lardner, Jr., the scriptwriter, and Altman from the book's layman-oriented descriptiveness to an ambiance of civilized carnage, of expediency and humanity steeped in self-preserving black humor and practicality. Near-pointless conversations are woven into the texture of complex surgery; assignations are made; Duke comments that he can't do anything with a situation because: "It looks like the Mississippi River down there." Hawkeye asks a nurse for a tool, not to aid in the amputation he's performing, but so that she can scratch his nose.

The ever ready Dago Red (Father Mulcahy, played by René Auberjonois) peers through the window and wanders tactfully among the OR (operating room) tables to see which cases may need his attention. But he's more useful as an unskilled assistant to Duke, who wants him to hold a retractor instead of administering the last rites. "I'm sorry, Dago, but this man is alive and the other one's dead, and that's a fact."

Trapper tells one girl, "You have a nice body, nurse. Otherwise we'd get rid of you quick," a comment on the value of competence temporarily being outweighed by

The emergency tent

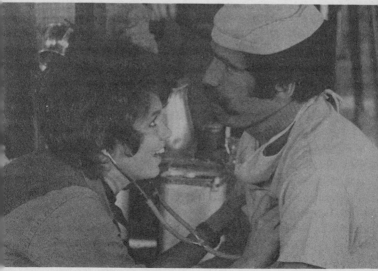

Jo Ann Pflug as Lieutenant Dish tests out a new stethoscope on Gould

aesthetic considerations. Another surgeon asks if anyone knows whether their subject is an officer or an enlisted man. When told the latter, the doctor orders, "Make the stitches bigger," to save time. The men aren't really callous; they just haven't time or energy to cope with more than their assigned ablations. They use so-called "black humor" to save their sanity, preferring to face the river of blood, the swabs and instruments, the cases that end in death anyway, and the surgery that isn't completely successful—the arm that can't be saved—to cracking up.

The OR is such an integral part of everyone's life that the head of the camp (Colonel Henry Blake, played by Roger Bowen) thinks nothing of introducing Hot Lips, the new chief nurse, to the staff as they're operating. Various personnel look up, say "Hi," or ignore the major, who smiles and salutes maniacally because that's what she's supposed to do. One nurse tries to shake hands with bloody gloves in midoperation, but gives up.

When the power fails and flashlights and lanterns are brought out so the operation can proceed, OR personnel spontaneously begin singing "When the Lights Go on Again All Over the World" and continue their conversations, related and unrelated to surgery. One vignette shows "Radar" O'Reilly (Gary Burghoff) tapping the colonel for his A-negative blood. The colonel mumbles, "Not now dear, go back to sleep," thinking it's his nurse/concubine, Lt. Leslie (Indus Arthur) wanting to make love. "We found a donor," Radar explains, shrugging off his effort, when asked how he found this rare commodity. Power failures, shortages of blood, incompetent or undertrained surgeons and orderlies are only a few of the many obstacles faced by those who are ready, willing, and able to do their jobs with a compliant wit and with what, on inspection, turns out to be a

*Elliott Gould nurses his fist after punching Robert Duvall;
Roger Bowen and Sally Kellerman at the door*

considerable amount of self-sacrifice.

Many viewers were so shocked or nonplussed by
Altman's cutting technique, not to mention the blood,
irreligiosity, and blithe fun in the face of trauma and
mayhem, that it took at least one additional viewing to
understand or appreciate what Altman and Lardner
were up to. As Vincent Canby said in the *New York
Times*, "The director has made a film so full of visual and
aural detail (each frame is packed with images from
foreground to back; the soundtrack is so busy it
sometimes sounds like three radio stations in one) that I'll
probably go back to see it again, to pick up what I missed

the first time."

Canby's fellow critic, Roger Greenspun, writing in the daily *Times*, was somewhat less pleased with the film: "*M* A* S* H* accepts without question several current pieties (for example, concern for a child's life, but not a grown man's soul), but its general bent is toward emotional freedom, cool wit, and shocking good sense.

"I think that *M* A* S* H*, for all its local virtues, is not successful. Its humor comes mostly in bits and pieces, and even in its climax, an utterly unsporting football game between the MASH unit and an evacuation hospital, it fails to build toward either significant confrontation or recognition. At the end, the film simply runs out of steam, says goodbye to its major characters, and calls final attention to itself as a movie—surely the saddest and most overworked of cop-out devices in the comic film repertory."

David Denby, writing in the *Atlantic Monthly*, took yet another stance: "*M* A* S* H* is the breakthrough in the realm of popular culture that *The Graduate* was supposed to be and really wasn't; its great achievement is to establish an acceptable heroism.... Its heroes are really something to admire. Carnal and witty, chivalrous but not soft, these men do something in the world with pride and success and have graciously retained the wildness of adolescence. Only the most unimaginative standards would find them disappointing; doubtless they aren't 'mature'—that insulting, coercive notion which requires us to give up so much to succeed."

Critical acceptance or disagreement aside, when all is said and done, the 4077th MASH that the film depicts is a well-trained and proficient unit, as is repeatedly, if briefly, demonstrated. Altman cuts directly from Major Burns leaving in a straitjacket to blood spurting from a patient's

The arrival of Hot Lips Houlihan

jugular vein as Hawkeye calmly gives instructions as to how the staff should proceed while holding his hands on the open wound. He then brags about the "fancy stitching" he'll use for the arterial suture. The attitude is: "It's all in a day's work."

One scene that most clearly depicts the precipitating influence of the war, and the possiblity of making a wrong diagnosis, takes place as a jumbled close-up of probing hands, retractors, tubes, scissors, suction devices and blood bottles with the doctors' voices heard discussing the case. Hawkeye and Trapper find the problem located where they didn't expect it. Hawkeye argues "to close him up and sit on him for a couple of days," then operate in the right place. Trapper John, in an Altmanesque line reflecting the gambling-with-lives atmosphere that prevails, says do it now—"We gotta shoot crap." There's not always enough time to make sure they're right, and besides, the wounded are piling up in the makeshift pre-op room.

Hawkeye and Trapper's trip to Japan to save the life of a congressman's wounded son is in no way different. The boys are on the helicopter landing hill practicing their golf, and seize the opportunity to leave the 4077th. "How many times do you get to go to Japan with your golf clubs? C'mon, Shirley," Trapper says, grabbing Hawkeye's arm and waltzing him away. The self-styled "pros from Dover" carry on in the same vein entering the hospital. Trapper John threatens an objecting WAC with his umbrella, and they continue to blast their way through the wards, barking orders and cowing the female staff into letting them have their own way. As Trapper remarks, "Give me at least one nurse who knows how to work in close without getting her tits in my way"—his personal metaphor for nursing skill. The pros discover, in the course of cracking the kid's chest, that their anesthetist is none other than Hawkeye's old pal from medical school, Me Lay Marston (Michael Murphy) who introduces himself by objecting slightly to the Hawk's collegiate humor: "So why don't you save your rapierlike wit for the clam diggers back home, Hawkeye?"

The next sequence, in which the doctors save the life of a Japanese-American baby born to one of the girls at the combination whorehouse and hospital where Me Lay moonlights, sounds a slightly wrong note. They're a bit too good to be true as they use the same high-handed methods to commandeer the army OR again and fix the infant's tracheo-esophageal fistula, with Hawkeye stating, "We don't want him, but we don't feel we can back away from him." They're becoming supermen, or knights in slightly tarnished armor, but they weren't presented in this light at first. If this is Denby's chivalrousness without softness, it's not a success.

The last operating-room scene, while typical of the attitudes that have preceded it, also rings false, as Hawkeye, breathless with the news that he and Duke have been rotated home, bursts into the OR to inform Forrest. While visions of his homecoming dance in Duke's head and Hawkeye gapes bemusedly in the door, another doctor asks rancorously, "Do you mind if we get out of this guy's brain first?" It's too glib and too fast, even for these quick-witted medics.

The film's second, less obvious, unifying force is "Radar" O'Reilly, who, from the beginning, anticipates his colonel's and everyone else's wishes and fulfills them quietly and efficiently. The book explains his prescience with a nod toward ESP, concentration and "certain atmospheric, as well as metabolic, conditions," but in the film he's simply a short, babyfaced, very bright and self-effacing young man. (Gary Burghoff has made a career of playing Radar. He's the only actor from the movie in the cast of the long-running TV show.)

Radar is absolutely unflusterable, reasonable, and adept. Even more than the principals, who occasionally fly off the handle, Radar typifies the sanity within the controlled chaos that is *M* A* S* H.* Whether placing a microphone under Hot Lips's cot as she enjoys loud, fervent sex with Frank Burns, swiping blood from the colonel, or crossing his fingers at the Painless Pole, recumbent in his coffin, Radar is cool, the epitome of self-contained, but not casual, professionalism.

The camp's loudspeaker functions almost as another leading character, broadcasting bulletins about esoteric surgery being performed by staff doctors, cases of missing amphetamines, mangled Japanese radio versions of American songs, and blurbs, apparently culled from the original ads, for the camp movies, all of which are about World War II. The owner of the voice, which carries on night and day, is never seen, and his transmissions are routinely ignored. No one ever attends *When Willie Comes Marching Home* or *The Glory Brigade*, the officers preferring to play poker with Painless, drink martinis in the Swamp, or make time with the available nurses.

Colonel Henry Blake and Dago Red bumble around in their own private worlds, and as long as nothing intrudes too forcefully, they're quite happy. Father Mulcahy isn't insulted by being called Dago Red; he even refers to himself that way. He tries to be, and is, a meaningful part of camp life. He goes to Hawkeye with Painless's problem, but is unable to divulge much because he learned about it in the confessional. He's truly worried and caring, which Hawkeye appreciates; hence his

Trapper John, Hawkeye, and Spearchucker (Fred William-son)

comforting pat on Dago's head as he exits to "see a man about a tooth." He's useful; he fills in the holes when needed, as in the scene where he holds the retractor for Duke. But he's not really with it; things usually have to be explained to him twice, as Hawkeye does when Painless is about to commit suicide. Pierce has to tell him Painless won't make it, "You're only dealing with an intention," that if the "last supper" succeeds, they will have prevented a mortal sin. Dago Red's confused as usual, but he gives Painless absolution as requested.

René Auberjonois, as Dago, wanders around reading his missal, one earflap on his cap up, the other down, his face as open and guileless here as it is closed and sneaky a year later in *McCabe and Mrs. Miller*. He believes the nighttime gathering in the colonel's office is listening to the radio and beats a hasty, flustered retreat when he realizes they've got Hot Lips in the sack, not the "Battling Bickersons." Dago Red, wondering what the line-up in front of the showers is for, withdraws, looking over his shoulder, and spots Hot Lips's "revelation" just in time to cover Ho-Jon's eyes from the contaminating sight.

But when it comes to other team sports, Dago Red is there waving his flag with the best of them as the 4077th takes the football game. He opens champagne cheerily in the locker room and, not long after, blesses the jeep that will carry Hawkeye and Duke away. Is he an addled clown, a little fey, or just dazed by his surroundings? Whatever the answer, he's there and welcome at all gatherings, including the cocktail hour. He's very much a part of the 4077th.

Not so Colonel Blake, who could leave at almost any time and not be missed, except perhaps for his surgical skills. Sergeant Major Vollmer (David Arkin) can run around with papers like a "Regular Army clown," and Radar can run the unit as he does anyway. The men circumvent the colonel, ignore his orders, and pretty much have things their own way, a fact Henry becomes aware of whenever his attention is diverted from tying complicated fish lures, going fishing, or playing house with his favorite nurse.

He permits Hawkeye and Duke to wangle Frank out of "their" tent although Major Burns was there first, but later protests, telling the boys he's tired of their running his outfit. It makes no difference; it suits them to run the unit, up to a point, so they continue to do so. Colonel Blake isn't totally inept; he just likes the easy way out. When Hot Lips bursts into his tent after her humiliation in the shower and threatens to resign, his response is a somewhat nonplussed, "Well, goddamn it, Hot Lips, resign your goddamn commission," followed by, "A little more wine, my dear?" to his bed partner. Old Henry just isn't touched by too much, and the thought that he might lose a good chief nurse never enters his head.

Told by Sergeant-Major Vollmer about Hot Lips's nocturnal public-address transmission, which happened while he was away ("There was nothing I could do about it."), Henry shrugs off the incident with: "Well, it couldn't have been helped." He fumbles around football practice, generally making a fool of himself, and commits a faux pas regarding Spearchucker's color. (Altman clearly likes these asides, which make his characters all the more human, and reprised this one in the speedway sequence of *Nashville*. Barbara Baxley has to restrain Henry Gibson from offering Timothy Brown watermelon and hands him lettuce instead, glaring at Gibson in reproof.) But during the game he's on his toes, calling Hot Lips and her cheerleaders "blithering idiots" when they cheer for the wrong thing or think the referee's gun means one of their players has been shot. He keeps a myopic eye on the proceedings and wisely leaves the running of the game to their pro.

In many ways the football sequence is not a success. It comes at the end of a long string of episodes filled with skullduggery and outrageousness, and is simply a final blast at the viewer's sensibilities. It's full of the truth of human behavior; it's crooked, raunchy, and fun. But the sequence is too much, and ultimately reveals itself to be a series of one-liners: the cheerleaders screaming "Sixty-nine is divine," when that player makes a point, an opponent knocked out of the game with an injection, the opposition smoking pot on the bench. The 4077th may win in a squeak, but they win, they're heroes, and it doesn't quite work.

Henry may be a bit thick, but his cranial density is certainly matched centimeter for centimeter by his other aide, the sergeant-major, and, like the colonel, he's out of step. He never quite succeeds at anything he sets out to do. Vollmer is the player Spearchucker elects to carry the ball for the final, triumphant, "semi-eligible" play of the game. He's so confused as he walks down the field toward the goal posts that he takes the ball from under his shirt and shows it to Henry, who tells him, against Spearchucker's orders, to run. Vollmer does, and is almost stopped by the opposition, but winds up in the safety zone, helplessly, hopelessly confessing his victory by holding the ball aloft. The sergeant-major isn't "one of the boys," he's a klutz, and neither Lardner, Altman, nor M*A*S*H's other characters waste any time on him.

If Colonel Blake and the sergeant-major are related by being mentally absent, Hot Lips and Frank are comparable through the force of their similar presences. They're both paranoid obsessives—paranoid with some reason, but obsessive by choice and personality.

The first sight of Major Houlihan introduces the 4077th MASH to her long legs, topped by her not unattractive body, exiting the helicopter which brings her to the camp. It's typical that the welcome committee, led by Henry, is expectantly facing the wrong way, and the copter approaches them from the rear. Hot Lips first runs into Major Burns, whom she admires for no apparent reason, then into Hawkeye, who sizes her up, while telling her that Frank is an "idiot, flipped his wig," as a "Regular Army clown," and leaves her fuming.

It doesn't take long for the two majors to find and comfort each other. They manage to combine lust and duty by embracing avidly after jointly composing a letter to General Hammond (G. Wood) complaining of lax procedures. Frank inspects Hot Lips's figure with the aid of a hanging light, they fall into each other's arms, groping, twisting, and sighing; then Hot Lips straightens up, pats her clothes into place, and is all business again while Frank, his face smeared with her lipstick, wonders what hit him. They're characterized by their dishonesty, which is limned as swiftly as the rest of the MASH company's attributes are. *M*A*S*H* was the first of Altman's panoramic studies of a special group assembled in a particular time and space for a definite purpose, and relates most directly to *Nashville* and *Buffalo Bill and the Indians*, although *McCabe and Mrs. Miller* bears a certain similarity.

As their characters are developed, it's logical that Hot Lips and the major would lie to themselves and one another instead of making a straightforward assignation. Frank arranges to return later, whereon they continue to evade the issue of why they're together. Hot Lips, tossing her head nervously, offers licorice; Frank calls the men who deride her "godless buffoons," while she quickly undoes her pajama top. Frank mumbles "God meant us to find each other"—as a means of excusing his marital infidelity, then falls on Hot Lips with a mixture of carnality and religious fervor only he could manage, as she exclaims, "His will be done!" Radar places the mike under her cot, and soon everyone's enjoying Hot Lips's sex life—and Major Margaret Houlihan's new name. Totally shattered by the experience of being bugged, the next day she has to endure the boys' gibes (Hawkeye to Trapper: "I think it's one of those ladies' things.") in the mess, where she nearly comes unglued. Trapper and Hawkeye are cruel, not because Hot Lips was caught in the sack, but because she's a hypocrite. You can do almost anything in the 4077th MASH except be stupid, lie, or get caught in stupidity or lying. If you're caught, you're fair game. Duke, referring to Frank's forced departure, sums up the incident by asking Henry: "Fair's fair. If I nail Hot Lips and punch Hawkeye out, do I get to go home?"

While the audience is allowed to sympathize a little with Hot Lips, Frank Burns gets no pity. From the moment Duke and Hawkeye find him giving Bible instruction to Ho-Jon, and quickly substitute a girlie magazine for the Psalms, to the occasion of Frank's accusing Boone (Bud Cort) of responsibility for a soldier's death (caused by Frank's ineptitude), for which Trapper knocks him down, the major is the target. He represents total hypocrisy, he's a bad doctor, and, apparently, he's crazy. In the mess, Hawkeye goes to work on Burns, asking if Hot Lips is better than self-abuse, and any pity one might feel for Frank as the butt of Pierce's attack is undercut by his mumbling his angry reply through a mouthful of breakfast. Frank assaults the Hawk, there's a scuffle, and the loudspeaker plays "Sayonara" as Frank disappears forever in a straitjacket.

But Hot Lips is still there, and gradually, she's assimilated into MASH life in a manner the film doesn't really make clear. It's a safe assumption that one or two scenes on the cutting room floor explain Hot Lips's transformation into a "good guy." First Trapper John tells her, "Hot Lips, you may be a pain in the ass, but you're a damned good nurse," then Trapper and Hawkeye spot Duke slipping her out the back of the Swamp on their return from Japan. She's humanized by being a bedmate, even a furtive one, for a member of the camp elite; next, Hot Lips is a cheerleader and, although she

may be an idiotic one, she couldn't fulfill this function without being accepted. Wearing a MASH T-shirt, she's seated on the arm of Duke's chair watching him play poker, and she's last seen assisting him in the operation Hawkeye interrupts. She's a major character like Hawkeye, Duke, and Trapper, the only one who changes in the course of the film, and the way in which her shift is accomplished should not be a mystery. As Vincent Canby put it: "Such nastiness demands consistency to be fully acceptable. 'Hot Lips' is a good deal more vulnerable than the men who torment her, but the odd and disturbing suspicions that *M*A*S*H*'s good guys are essentially bastards are dropped (unfortunately, I feel) in favor of conventional sentiment. 'Hot Lips' is apparently transformed into one of the girls.... The movie itself trails off, having abandoned its dark premises in favor of easy laughs."

Sally Kellerman remembers getting the script from Altman: "I was there to see about the role of Lieutenant Dish, and I think I had hold of his pants leg or something because he took a long look at me and jumped up and yelled, *'Hot Lips!'* I just said, 'Oooh, yes! Hot Lips!' Then I looked at it. It was about three pages long. I told Bob Altman I hated him ... and they could all take their stupid little project and go screw themselves. Bob Altman said, 'Don't worry, I plan to make up this movie as we go along. You've got to be Hot Lips. We'll try things. They'll work.'" Then later: "Hot Lips changed me because she was the only character in the film who was allowed to change.... She ended up *gaining* from the degradation.... She was a pill, but she ended up part of

(previous page) An impromptu golf game

the family. . . . I would do anything for Bob Altman."

Kellerman's hero, Altman, almost didn't get to direct *M* A* S* H*. As Aljean Harmetz reported in the *New York Times*, "Robert Altman had waited 20 years for the historical accident of having 14 *more acceptable* directors turn down *M* A* S* H*." Donald Sutherland, who got top billing and the largest role in the film, had the same doubts that Twentieth Century-Fox did that Altman was the right director for the film. Part way through the filming, he and Elliott Gould tried to have him removed, but when *M* A* S* H* was a hit, both men, especially Gould, gave Altman credit for boosting their careers. The reviews generally praised the ensemble acting, but Greenspun of the *Times* objected to Sutherland's handling of Hawkeye: "Donald Sutherland (in a very elaborate performance) supports his kind of detachment with vocal mannerisms that occasionally become annoying."

Nonetheless, Sutherland's impression of Hawkeye Pierce does work as an individual character and as part of the whole. Altman places him immediately in context by showing Hawkeye arriving on his way to the MASH unit on the right side of the screen while Gen. Douglas MacArthur's farewell address appears superimposed on the left: "I have left your fighting sons in Korea. [They] are splendid in every way. . . ." succeeded by Dwight Eisenhower's campaign promise: "I will go to Korea." Hawkeye, the splendid son's first act (he later addresses his "dad" for a roving moviemaker) is to "borrow" a jeep to take himself and fellow captain, Duke Forrest, who thinks he's a driver, to the 4077th. "I'd follow you anywhere, sir," Hawkeye says cheerily, and off they go.

Besides Hawkeye's breezy self-confidence, the other

Trapper and Hawkeye make an instant diagnosis

part of his persona that is quickly introduced is the whistle, *"Whoo eee woo,"* which Greenspun found annoying and which Hawkeye used to punctuate his reactions to even the most mundane communications. This whistle is like the talking to themselves that many other characters from then on, Gould in *The Long*

Goodbye, Gould and George Segal in *California Split*, Barbara Harris in *Nashville*, and Paul Newman in *Buffalo Bill* indulge in. Altman has solved the problem Shakespeare dealt with when he had his people address the audience directly. What "real" human beings say to themselves, Altman's individuals say out loud, and they make it seem natural, not an imposed device designed to give plot or character clues away without any exposition. Shelley Duvall's diary in *3 Women* is a form of talking to herself.

Hawkeye immediately becomes a part of the company, instructing Ho-Jon in drink mixing, insisting on the informality of being called "Hawkeye" rather than Captain Pierce, ridiculing Frank Burns, and finally driving him around the bend and out of the camp. He masterminds Painless's suicide and recovery in a MASH-wide conspiracy to rescue the Pole from his delusion. The "last supper" he arranges may be a travesty, but it serves its purpose and the song which accompanies the meal and the farewells is a classic of cool, the delineation of the high-stakes, winner-take-nothing game that is both war and life:

> The game of life is hard to play.
> I'm going to lose it anyway.
> The losing card I'll someday lay,
> So this is all I have to say.
> The only way to win is cheat....

(These lyrics were written by Altman's teenaged son Mike, and set to music by Johnny Mandel.)

Painless accepts the "black capsule," a tranquilizer decked out as lethal goods, and climbs into his coffin to accept his buddies' farewells. He gets a bottle of Scotch, his three sweethearts' pictures, crossed fingers, and a parting shot from Private Boone, the admonition that "You're throwing your whole education away." His attempts to seduce Lieutenant Dish having been unsuccessful, Hawkeye settles for turning her over to the "dead" Pole, "the best equipped dentist in the army," in a "tender act of mercy," which brings Painless back to life and sends Lieutenant Dish home to the husband she swore she'd never cheat on with a smile on her face.

Although Hawkeye scorns sham, he's not above using it, mostly in fun, as a device to get what *he* wants. He and Trapper are faking their insolence at the hospital in Japan. They're putting Me Lay, the staff, and Colonel Merrill on with their demands, and they get away with it by force of personality, threats of bodily harm, and by simply being different from everyone else. They prevail and they save a baby. Lardner and Altman inflate the activities of Hawkeye, Trapper, and Me Lay into the tactics of supermen; they're heroic white rescuers of a sick, biracial infant, and although their motives are the best, and the sequence is funny (audiences love to see pompous bureaucrats laid low, whether via logic or anesthesia), it's excessive. *M*A*S*H* doesn't need this to make its point about moral idiots, doctor/saviors and military small-mindedness.

But Hawkeye isn't shamming with Lieutenant Dish. He wants to take her to bed in the worst way, and he's completely honest with her. "If my wife were here, I'd be doing this with her," he declares as he hauls the lieutenant down on a table and becomes enmeshed in her sweater.

Hawkeye, Trapper, and Duke are human heroes, not antiheroes, but part of the time Lardner and Altman don't seem to have made up their minds which direction they want their characters to take. Inconsistency, am-

Trapper and Hawkeye are chauffeured by Sergeant Gorman (Bobby Troup)

bivalence, and frailty are human attributes, and Altman and Lardner appear to want these three to be as human as possible; instead they're almost cartoons, life-sized cartoons with no doubts that their means, no matter how heinous, are justified by the ends. For the rest of the film, the director and author are on surer ground with the medical captains, and their behavior springs from personalities that have some basis in reality, at least the reality of the 4077th MASH.

If the conduct of Hawkeye, Trapper, and Duke is an attempt to retain their sanity within the madness of war, clearly they are successful. Outside the OR they construct a world that operates, and looks like, a grubby country club, complete with a cocktail hour, sports, practical jokes, helping friends, getting rid of troublesome members, and grabbing sex whenever an opportunity presents itself. And they make everyone their accomplices, from Radar and the colonel to Dago Red and Lieutenant Dish, right through to Hot Lips Houlihan. Nobody questions their right to carry on in this manner, least of all the film itself, which wholly endorses its characters' actions; nor does any opprobrium (except that expressed by Frank and Hot Lips, who, being square, don't count) attach itself, even to their less admirable exertions.

Hawkeye plays it loose; he's not too deeply involved, and like his buddies he survives his Korean experience. Survival, at whatever the cost to others, is the name of the game in *M*A*S*H*'s idea of war. Dago Red supplies the most accurate assessment of Hawkeye when, responding to Hot Lips's question of how a degenerated person like that ever reached a position of responsibility in the army: "He was drafted."

Being from the North, Trapper John and Hawkeye are medical soul brothers, but their friendship doesn't exclude Duke; they simply have more in common with each other than with the Southerner. Duke's around, taking bets on Hot Lips's hair color, playing football, rooming with "that nigra boy," Spearchucker, and turning out not to be as prejudiced as he thought. Duke isn't a real oddball, so he pales in comparison to the gaudy personalities the other two flash around.

Trapper John McIntyre arrives as the unit's much needed chest-cutter, and is a self-made mystery man to boot. Ensconced in the Swamp, he smiles enigmatically as Hawkeye tells him, "I've seen your face before, stranger," but even Hawkeye shuts up, completely flummoxed, when Trapper produces a jar from the recesses of his parka and, plopping one into his drink, comments, "A martini isn't a martini without an olive."

The riddle of Trapper's identity is solved during an impromptu football session, but there's no explanation of why there should have been a mystery in the first place. Hawkeye explains how Trapper got his name: "He's the only man who ever found fulfillment in the ladies' can of the Boston and Maine railway"—he trapped the object of his desire there.

In an atmosphere that thrives on cool, the three Swampmen are the coolest. It's this commodity Trapper exhibits in quantity during his stay in Korea. After punching Frank out in the supply room for maltreating Private Boone, he's told by Colonel Blake that he's under arrest. Trapper ignores Blake and brushes by the hapless non-com attempting to carry out Blake's order, saying "Are you kidding?" Trapper knows he's indispensable, and he isn't going to let anyone get in his way; he has a sense of justice—or, at least, the sense not to let an inexcusable injustice go unpunished.

Like his confreres, Trapper knows a target when he sees one. First it's Frank, then Hot Lips. During a party, Trapper, wearing a paper hat and yelling, "I want sex!" is carried into the mess by his friends, who sing "Hail to the Chief" in his honor. He spots Hot Lips and hollers, "Bring me that sultry bitch, the one with the fire in her eyes." Hot Lips's gaze flickers with interest but, ever the hypocrite, nothing breaks her reserve.

For all the talk of Hawkeye and Trapper being Northeastern clam diggers, Elliott Gould plays Trapper in the mold of his earlier and later roles, as a New Yorker with lots of chutzpah. The approach works; Trapper John has enough gall and silly charm to divide into three parts. He sails through the Japanese hegira brandishing umbrellas, X rays, and a smart mouth that gets him into and out of trouble with a rapidity that surprises even himself. He helps Hawkeye plot Painless's suicide and plays in the football game. He and Hawkeye are the "pros from Dover" and they never let anyone forget it.

Visually, *M*A*S*H* represents a breakthrough for Altman. It looks the way all his films from then on would look—that is, the way he wanted them to. Altman's visuals are functional; they follow the form of the film and do not obtrude for purposes of decoration. In *M*A*S*H*, although the camera is very often in motion, the movement seldom calls attention to itself, being subtle and purposeful rather than flashy. One is most aware of camera placement in two scenes:

The first occurs as Major Burns wards off the evil influence personified by Hawkeye and Duke. He kneels by his cot, including "our Supreme Commander in the field and our Commander in Chief in Washington, D.C." in his prayers. At first, Hawkeye respects Frank's religious ardor by taking his hat off, but when Frank meanders on, he and Duke begin to put him on, asking "Were you always like this, or did you crack up over here?" and breaking into "Onward Christian Soldiers," which a group strolling past the tent joins in and marches along to. Dago Red thinks the hymn represents genuine religious fervor and smiles approvingly. Altman and his cinematographer, Harold E. Stine, achieve this complicated series of interactions in one take, moving from within the tent, in an extreme close-up of Frank's face, past Hawkeye and Duke, to the passersby joining in, to Dago glancing at the singers. They've depicted piety, no matter how fake, its mockery and the real thing, delineating and developing character in a brief traveling shot.

The second sequence takes place as Trapper's surgical team leaves the OR and runs into a football game. Trapper

*M*A*S*H poker*

steals the ball and runs around a tent as Hawkeye goes the other way, whistles, and catches the ball Trapper passes to him. Altman accomplishes the scene in one shot, starting on the ground facing the team, following the players' actions, then angling up into a crane shot that travels over the tent and back down to the ground as Hawkeye receives the ball. Whatever virtuosity the shot might have is undercut by the overall drabness of the locale, its mud and tents, the gloomy morning, and the fact that form has followed function. Altman wants more than to show some postsurgery high jinks; this is the scene in which Hawkeye remembers where he knows Trapper from—playing intercollegiate football against Hawkeye's school.

The rest of *M*A*S*H* is in the same visual mold, with Altman and Stine opting for monochromatic realism broken by occasional flashes of color—blood, the gaudy golf outfits Trapper and Hawkeye return from Japan in, or football jerseys—over anything more intrusive.

Although Lion's Gate 8-Track Sound wasn't developed when Altman made *M*A*S*H*, it might well have been. The lifelike overlapping dialogue Altman had always wanted and had been fired from television and *Countdown* for trying to achieve is officially born as a technique in *M*A*S*H*. It does sound like life, which is both an advantage and a disadvantage, the former because *M*A*S*H* is less like an ordinary movie than many other films that had been made until 1969, and more like life visually and audibly. The resulting auditory confusion means that often lines that one assumes may be important are lost as the character moves out of range mumbling and talking away from the camera. Unseen lip movements increase perplexity. It also has the effect Altman was striving for—to draw the audience into his films, to involve them and to force them to react emotionally to what's happening on screen. After a second or third viewing one realizes that, in fact, one has not missed any significant lines—the import was always there, and one did actually get it.

M* A* S* H is a film that takes friendly pot shots at totems it has long been fashionable to mock: religion, hypocrisy, the stupidity of war. Nothing much really changes within the time span of the film. Some people have been through and left the 4077th MASH a little better, or worse, for wear. There have been some laughs and some adventures, and a great deal of excellent surgery has been performed under adverse conditions. The 4077th is an episode in these individuals' lives, as the Korean conflict was an episode in that country's and America's history. And when it was over, it was over.

It was the form, the gleeful irreverence, the buckets of blood, more than the targets themselves, which aroused critical ire and audience joy. Seven years after its release M* A* S* H is still funny, and still in many ways a trail blazer, but that's the dull thumping of old fists on a well-worn target one hears, not the rat-tat-tat of machine gun fire on fresh ground.

The long-running, half-hour-a-week television series developed from the film after M* A* S* H was a hit has very little to do with the movie. In its way, it's closer to Hooker's novel; the characters are softer and have degenerated into sit-com sweetness from their first TV appearance, when they were slightly more acerbic. Wayne Rogers played Trapper, but he left the series and Alan Alda's Hawkeye has a second sidekick played by Mike Farrell. The Colonel Blake character (McLean Stevenson) has become the crusty but lovable Colonel Potter (Harry Morgan). Loretta Swit plays Hot Lips, now usually called Margaret, and Radar (Gary Burghoff) and

Frank Burns (Larry Linville), a paranoid clown, are still on the scene. Klinger, a Greek non-com masquerading as a transvestite to obtain his discharge, is a fairly recent addition and an example of the direction the TV *M*A*S*H*, under the guidance of producer-director Gene Reynolds, has taken.

Brewster McCloud

Brewster McCloud, the first film Altman made after the enormous success of *M*A*S*H*, was taken from Doran William Cannon's original screenplay, called *Brewster McCloud's Flying Machine*. Cannon, who gets sole screenplay credit for the film, compiled a list of his complaints for the *New York Times* about what Altman had done to *his* film. He felt that his "vision" had been violated by Altman and producer Lou Adler, but he didn't take his name off the film. C. Kirk McClelland, at the time a cinema student at the University of Southern California, followed the company around Houston during the shooting. His diary was published as *On Making a Movie: Brewster McCloud*, and contains cast sketches, an organizational breakdown, a graph of production responsibility, a daily journal which is the largest portion of the book, an afterword, and the shooting script and Cannon's original screenplay.

In the journal McClelland chronicles the firing of Jordan Cronenweth, a young cinematographer, and the arrival of Lamar Boren, who completed the film, and various incidents that occurred during the shooting: Altman's anger at Sally Kellerman, who kept the crew waiting while she fiddled with her makeup; Bud Cort, the young star, who didn't know how to drive and kept

Margaret Hamilton as Daphne Heap in BREWSTER McCLOUD

banging up the limousine he was supposed to chauffeur Stacy Keach around Houston in; problems with the Houston Astrodome representatives, and so on.

During the filming, Altman and some of his company were invited to the engagement party of Shelley Duvall and Bernard Sampson, Jr., the young color-blind artist she married and divorced four years later. Altman immediately cast Duvall as the tour guide and first sexual contact of Bud Cort, who betrays him. Duvall went on to make more films with Altman, who was the only director who could find any way of using her offbeat looks until Joan Micklin Silver cast her in *Bernice Bobs Her Hair* and Woody Allen gave her a small part in *Annie Hall* (1977).

Bud Cort clumsily engineers the wheelchair of 120-year-old Stacy Keach

The cast of *Brewster* includes seven members of the cast of *M*A*S*H*: Bud Cort, Sally Kellerman, Michael Murphy, John Schuck, Corey Fischer, G. Wood, and René Auberjonois. Kellerman plays Brewster's fairy birdmother Louise, a sort of guardian angel with wing scars on her back, Murphy is Frank Shaft, a humorless cop imported from San Francisco (his role is modeled on Sidney Poitier's in *In the Heat of The Night* and Steve McQueen's in *Bullitt*), and John Schuck plays a dumb Houston traffic cop who ferries Shaft around in a police car and can't remember to call him Frank. Auberjonois is a maniacal lecturer on birds whose appearance and behavior become more bizarre as the film progresses, G. Wood is a cranky head cop modeled on the same profane sort of character he played in *M*A*S*H*, and Corey Fischer is another cop who lusts after the bruised widow of rotten detective Bert Remsen, killed early in the movie.

In spite of everyone's good intentions and some very nice performances, *Brewster McCloud* ranks as one of Altman's interesting failures. It's hard to pinpoint why, except that the central conceit of the film does not seem to have been strong enough to bear all the weight Altman's concept wanted it to.

Brewster is a young *naïf* who lives in a bomb shelter in the Houston Astrodome constructing his wings, with which he will "fly away." He is aided and abetted by Hope (Jennifer Salt), who steals health food from the store where she works and worships Brewster to the point of having orgasms while concealed under a blanket as he does chin-ups to strengthen his arm muscles. His other benefactress is Louise, who steals too—cameras, whatever Brewster needs to carry on his work—bathes him, warns him away from sex, and commits murder whenever Brewster is threatened. The Houston stranglings are the events that make it necessary to call in Shaft. Although the first murder we see is that of Daphne Heap, the rich old crone who sings the national anthem in the Astrodome and who dies wearing Dorothy's red slippers from *The Wizard of Oz* (she's played by Margaret Hamilton, who was the Wicked Witch of the West in that film), there have been earlier deaths. Next to go is Mr. Wright, Brewster's venal employer, who owns a string of rundown nursing homes named after birds. There are others in the course of the film. Shaft, toward the end of the film, after a slam-bang chase through Houston, ends up in a pond with both legs broken and shoots himself. Murphy recalls how this came about: "I wound up committing suicide. I had no idea I was going to do that

Sally Kellerman pays a visit to Bud Cort

Bud Cort as Brewster

Jennifer Salt as Brewster's freaky girlfriend

till the day before I did it. We had dinner together the night before, and he said, 'I've got this great idea.' I said, 'Jesus, I'd like to have known that ten weeks ago.' I didn't like that idea, and we argued about it as much as you argue with him when he decides that's what he's going to do. I said that I thought it was a real depressing thing. He took a real strong attitude about it. Maybe he was right. I don't know about that point."

The last death is that of Haskell Weeks (William Windom) the nerd politician whose idea it was to bring Shaft to Houston. Weeks, as well as all the other characters, points the way toward the conceptual problem in *Brewster McCloud*—they're all stereotypes: McCloud, the fey innocent and genius inventor; Louise, the luscious, loving guru; Shaft, the supercool detective; Hope, the repressed hero worshipper; Breen, the brutal, stupid cop; Johnson, the dumb but nice cop; Wright, the greedy, bawdy Howard Hughes of the nursing-home business; Weeks, the politician who's so busy figuring angles he can't see the problem; Suzanne, the temptress who is the hero's undoing; Daphne Heap, the vicious society grande dame; and the maniacal lecturer who becomes his own subject. The ending, which occurs after Brewster has successfully flown, takes place as a circus invades the arena and ignores Brewster's crumpled body and wings in the middle of the Astrodome. The cast members, dressed as circus-type personifications of their parts, come on and are introduced, a la the ending of *M*A*S*H*, by their real names. It's a Felliniesque ending and, considering what has preceded it, is as successful as any other aspect of the film.

The problems certainly do not arise from the fact that Altman didn't make Cannon's screenplay. The original is a more literal version of what Altman has

John Schuck as Lieutenant Johnson

filmed, and in many ways it's pretty silly. Altman clearly wanted to make several statements about contemporary American life, about marriage and about "hippies" and "flower children," those human artifacts of the sixties whose time was just about over. His views on the fatuity of politics and the corruption of business are the same in *Brewster* as they are in *McCabe and Mrs. Miller.* Certainly the parts played by Windom in the former and William DeVane in the latter are very much alike, and Keach in *Brewster* is an older individual version of the company representatives played by Murphy and Anthony Holland in *McCabe.*

Altman does not seem to have been able to grasp any kind of unifying idea about what he wanted to do. As a character Brewster is so elusive he practically skitters off the screen. Lacking this center, a really interesting focal personage, Altman has to concentrate on building up interest in the characters around Brewster, but then he's in a catch-22 situation. These individuals have no nucleus to cohere *around.* So he uses the screen time to develop subsidiary stories relating to the havoc Brewster's obsession causes, side trips where the action can go when Brewster is off screen: Louise stealing film, Shaft's arrival in Houston, Shaft in the police lab checking the birdshit specimens scraped off each of Louise's victims (a poster for a film, *The Decline and Fall of a Bird Watcher*, a 1969 flop, is tacked to the lab door; at this point it's hard not to agree with Roger Greenspun's criticism of *M*A*S*H* in deploring films which refer to themselves as films), or G. Wood and his wife, and Corey Fischer and Remsen's widow, having their picture taken in the park when Shaft's car goes into the pond. But all of this furious activity cannot disguise the fact that it's done in the service of a very slight idea: that innocents and dreamers

Shelley Duvall and Bud Cort

should be protected and allowed to flourish, even at the
expense of society at large, and that those who stand in
their way are purveyors of corruption.

Vincent Canby of the *New York Times* said that
"*Brewster McCloud* has more characters and incidents
than a comic strip, but never enough wit to sustain more
than a few isolated sequences. The original screenplay by
Doran William Cannon [has] to do with elaborate
conspiracies and attempt[s] to define the American scene
in terms of satire that is not exactly of the first freshness."
Andrew Sarris, of the *Village Voice* disagreed: "Robert
Altman's direction here is so admirably controlled in
tempo and rhythm that no satiric conceit ever gets out of
hand. For example, Michael Murphy's ridiculously
stoical suicide is literally (and visually) distanced by
Altman's cool cutting and disjunctive landscape work
with some Texas Gothic types."

Brewster takes flight

Pauline Kael wrote in the *New Yorker*, "The picture has a demoralized melancholy, yet silly tone; it isn't noisy, but it's somewhat manic. It's disconnected in a way that could be explained as social comment or as a new, free style, but I don't think it is either. Altman has a distinctive use of overlapping sound, and the track sometimes has an independent life; and he has a distinctive sense of film rhythm. But the individual sequences don't reveal what they're for—they can be taken almost any way—and when they're all put together the picture has no driving impulse and no internal consistency. The ambiguities (such as whether Brewster or the fallen-angel-lady or a mysterious crow commits the murders) seem more like a form of indecision than like purposeful ambiguity. And yet it all appears to be done with considerable directorial confidence—as if Altman didn't know the gags were schoolboy humor, the characterization vague, and the dialogue a shambles. Most of the members of the cast are weak—probably because they are playing almost unwritten roles, and the gaps haven't been plugged by improvisation. When an actor is supposed to parody a Steve McQueen hotshot San Francisco police detective but is given almost nothing to work with except the repeated exclamation 'Jesus Christ!' the effect isn't parody and it isn't comedy. It's like a rehearsal, with the actors just saying anything while waiting for the script to arrive."

Audiences couldn't make up their minds if they wanted to see the film any more than the critics could decide whether or not they could recommend *Brewster McCloud*, and it died at the box office. Altman had been hired by MGM to make the movie on the basis of

(previous page) Brewster aloft in the Houston Astrodome

The film's finale, with Sally Kellerman, Michael Murphy, and ring-master William Windom

M*A*S*H being a hit. He was supposed to do for antic American comedy and for MGM what Dennis Hopper's *Easy Rider* had done for road/youth movies and Columbia Pictures. But, as Universal learned to its sorrow when they gave Hopper a free hand and a huge budget to make *The Last Movie* in South America, lightning seldom strikes twice in the same place. Hopper struck out, but Altman's film was dumped by MGM because that studio lost confidence in what he was doing before the film was even completed. Michael Murphy commented on the phenomenon: "It was a picture that I think not only, I don't mean this by way of an excuse, but I do think it misses a lot of people, although I understand it's in the black now because people keep watching it. It keeps turning up, and it may not be a totally satisfying film, but it was really dumped by the studio with a vengeance. It was handled maliciously. It was almost as though they were going to get him. Everything broke

down between him and [James] Aubrey and the studio. I
think they were really trying to unload it. I really saw
studio politics working firsthand. It was kind of a sad
experience. I don't quite know what to say about the
picture itself... I like the film. I think it's very funny and
yes, I can sit in a screening room where people don't
understand it. Jesus, well, we had a lot of guts. And then
other times I feel really terrific about it because people
really like it or people come up to you in the street and say,
'Gee, you know I've seen that picture fifteen times.' But
again it's that thing of taking a chance and doing
something crazy and hoping for it to... I don't think it
just lies there like a lot of things. I think it's got real life to
it. I think it'll hold up. I think that picture's going to be
around."

McCabe and Mrs. Miller

Traveling lady, stay awhile until the night is over.
I'm just a station on your way, I know I'm not your lover.

Leonard Cohen's song, "Winter Lady," which Altman says subconsciously influenced his film, aptly describes John McCabe's relationship with Mrs. Constance Miller. Altman talks about how Cohen's songs found their way into his film: "I made a film called *That Cold Day in the Park* in Vancouver in 1968. That was about the time Leonard Cohen's first album came out. I got the album and I loved it. I played it and I wore it out and I bought another one. It was just constantly part of my life at that time. Then two years later when we went back to Vancouver to make *McCabe and Mrs. Miller*, it never occurred to me. I never consciously thought of Leonard Cohen. We had the music box, and I put one of the characters in as a fiddle player, and I had another as a flute player, and I was going to draw the music organically out of there, at least the basis for it. We finished the picture and I went to Paris just to warm up. We were sitting in a girl's apartment one night and she put on that Leonard Cohen album, and I said, 'Shit! That's my picture!' We left literally the next day, we flew back and transferred the stuff and put it in the picture. It fit so well. Then I realized

Cohen's music had influenced me in the rhythm of that picture and in the way the characters are developed. So then they said, 'It's impossible, because this is Warner Brothers and he's with Columbia.' So I called Cohen and fifteen minutes later it was worked out."

Altman, as usual, reduced his source material, in this case Edmund Naughton's novel *McCabe*, to a series of character sketches strung together with some connective plot threads. John McCabe (Warren Beatty) comes to the town of Presbyterian Church, somewhere in the Pacific Northwest, at the turn of the century with the idea of starting a combination gambling palace and whorehouse. He reasons that lonely men working in the town's zinc mine will be ready customers. McCabe is quickly joined by the enterprising Mrs. Miller (Julie Christie), herself a prostitute, who proposes to become his partner in the whorehouse operation and run the business for him. Both the zinc mine and McCabe's concern are extremely successful, and McCabe receives an offer from two representatives of Harrison & Shaughnessy, the zinc company, to sell out. A lawyer advises him that he doesn't have to sell, but it's too late. The company sends three hired killers to deal with McCabe. Mrs. Miller, with whom McCabe has been having a tentative affair, advises him to leave, but he decides to take them on. Mrs. Miller, an opium addict, slides into a drugged daze as McCabe, having prevailed against his would-be assassins, dies alone in the snow.

McCabe, like many of Altman's male protagonists, is something of a fool. He fancies himself a sport and a rough diamond among the dudes of Presbyterian Church, but he's a small-timer, and when Mrs. Miller comes on the scene, she spots him for what he is. In her kindly/harsh way, she tells him he'll make a better impression if he wears "something besides that cheap Jockey Club cologne." McCabe's affectations are many. He has a gold tooth, a bowler hat he takes good care of, a diamond stickpin, and a knack for at least the appearance of personal cleanliness, unshared by anyone in town until Mrs. Miller arrives with her bathhouse and penchant for making sure her girls are uninfected.

But Constance Miller is too much for McCabe. She breezes into his life on the back of the steam tractor that brings supplies and the mail-order bride of Bart Coyl (Bert Remsen), Ida (Shelley Duvall), to Presbyterian Church. She demands a meal, slurps it down with all the refinement of one of the zinc miners, and immediately states her offer. She has certain hygienic specifications which must be met (like the bathhouse the men have to visit before they can see her girls), and from which McCabe will be able to realize a profit. She'll be a madam and the highest priced hooker in the house for her cut, and McCabe can have everything else. McCabe was all right when he was small potatoes like Sheehan (René Auberjonois); his problems arise from his partnership with Mrs. Miller. She undermines his self-confidence without saying anything directly beyond nagging him ("I don't want no small-timer screwin' up me business"), and because, in his befuddled way, he has fallen in love with her. There's a lot of John McCabe in Altman's conception of *Buffalo Bill*. Both men drink, both men can't keep their women exactly happy, and both men have problems with the other people around them: Bill with his retinue of flacks and partners, McCabe with Sheehan (who tells people McCabe has a "big rep" because he killed Bill Roundtree) and with the zinc company's representatives who want to buy him out. But McCabe's principal difficulties lie in his deepening affections for Constance

Miller who, when she's full of opium, is pliant, smiling, and gentle, and thoroughly puts off McCabe, who's used to her roughness.

McCabe talks to himself, because he's lonely and because he has no close male friends to turn to. He talks when he's been drinking alone, and always it's about Constance. "Trouble and pain, that's what you give me, trouble and pain. . . . Freezin' my soul, that's what you're doin', just freezin' my soul," he tells himself. The fiddler (Brantley F. Kearns) who runs the gang working on McCabe's buildings—The House of Fortune, the whorehouse, and the bathhouse—keeps neat receipts, but McCabe, in his own words, "can't tell the goddamn owls from the chickens." Mrs. Miller can, and she turns up after the first day's work with a sewing box full of cash, apologizing because there's a small amount missing due to some opening-day confusion. Even then she wants McCabe to expand and reproves him bitterly, "You think small 'cause you're afraid to think big." She has the soul of a bookkeeper and a mind like a cash register.

Mrs. Miller is also thoroughly self-sufficient, despite her dependence on opium. One scene which shows McCabe, flowers in hand, talking to her through her locked door while she massages her feet and smiles at a book she's reading, delineates their whole relationship. She gets her way; he gets grief. Mrs. Miller's given name, Constance, is a misnomer. She's capable of affection, but spiritually absent when McCabe needs her. She has a tough exterior, but she isn't tough enough to be there when he's in trouble or in doubt. Once she lets him have sex with her without paying for it, but when she realizes

(previous page) Julie Christie and Warren Beatty as Mrs. Miller and McCabe

McCabe has met his match with the men from Harrison &
Shaughnessy's, she spends some time mooning around in
the snow, lost in thought, then cuts out for the Chinese
opium den. Vincent Canby of the *New York Times*
admired Altman's intentions in making *McCabe and
Mrs. Miller*, but felt that the director had failed to realize
many of them. He cited the handling of the ending as
having a "sort of metaphysically purposeful photography
that, in a tight close-up, attempts to discover the soul's
secrets in the iris of an eye and finds, instead, only a very
large iris." Otherwise he liked the film very much: "The
characters of *McCabe and Mrs. Miller* as written and as
played do have an essential dignity that is very real and
honest. They make a marvelously practical team and are
immensely successful until The Company moves to take
over their businesses."

Pauline Kael stated her enthusiasm for the film and for
Beatty and Christie in the *New Yorker*: "Altman brings
them into focus so unobtrusively that it's almost as if we
had sorted them out from the others by ourselves.
Without rigid guidelines, we observe them differently,
and as the story unfolds, Beatty and Christie reveal more
facets of their personalities than are apparent to us in
those star vehicles that sell selected aspects of stars to us.
[Julie Christie] is a weird, hounded beauty as the junkie
madam, Mrs. Miller—that great, fat underlip the only
flesh on her, and her gaunt emaciated face surrounded by
frizzy ringlets. She's like an animal hiding in its own fur.
When her nose practically meets her strong chin and she
gets the look of a harpy, the demonstration of the thin line
between harpy and beauty makes the beauty more
dazzling—it's always threatened. It is the depth in her that
makes her too much for the cocky, gullible McCabe; his
inexpressible poetry is charming but too simple. It's hard

to know what makes Beatty such a magnetic presence. . . . He has an unusually comic romantic presence; there's a gleefulness in Beatty, a light that comes on when he's on screen that says 'Watch this—it's fun.' . . . His best lines are between him and us. Beatty carries off this tricky yokel form of soliloquy casually, with good-humored self-mockery. It's a fresh, ingenuous performance; we believe McCabe when he says that Mrs. Miller is freezing his soul."

Mrs. Miller is, in many ways, another of Altman's characters who, without knowing quite how it happened, have reached the end of their tether. There's a desperation to her tenacity which says she thinks this is her last shot. If she doesn't make it in this backwater, she'll never get a chance anywhere else. She's like Robert Duvall's Major Burns in *M*A*S*H*, trying to shut the world out with prayer as she does with dope. We don't know why this should be so; we only know she must have gotten the idea to come to Presbyterian Church from hearing Beatty bargain for "chippies" with the whorehouse proprietor in Bear Paw; there was a brief glimpse of her in the door there. But why she's so determined to be a cold-hearted bitch, when anyone can see she's got the instincts of a mother hen, is left a mystery. She's cheerful and philosophical with Ida Coyl, who has to fall back on the oldest profession when her husband's death leaves her stranded in Presbyterian Church. She tells the frightened girl to relax, to "think of something else," and that, as a whore, she doesn't "have to ask nobody for nothing— more honest, to my mind." She helps with the preparations for a birthday party and generally brings whatever small refinements she can to the town.

But McCabe is a thick-headed gent, and for all his desperately glib chat—"I keep trying to tell you in a lot of different ways. I got poetry in me. I can't put it down on paper. I got sense enough not to try."—he has the soul of a small entrepreneur, which is what he is until Mrs. Miller turns him into an enormously successful merchant. She's the one who turns McCabe's limited aspirations into the whopping achievement they are. The awful irony is that without Mrs. Miller, McCabe would always be small potatoes, but he'd still be alive. She turns him into an obstacle whose property is so valuable it's worth killing him for, and when this happens, she's finished, too.

The town of Presbyterian Church is almost another character in the film, like the loudspeaker in *M*A*S*H.* Leon Ericksen built, as the film progressed, an impressively ugly, sprawling village, which mirrors in its unplanned unsightliness the systematic rape of the countryside that the zinc miners are perpetrating in pursuit of their own fortunes. But it's a curiously beautiful and affecting rape. From its first raw unfinished state, the town adds buildings, the church spire grows. Things seem to have *possibility* in Presbyterian Church, a chance that they wouldn't have if the town where they happened were already more complete. It's a fit place for McCabe and Mrs. Miller to try to realize their dreams. It's also the West, not exactly the wild West, since it's 1902, but still untamed and still an area where life is cheap. When Dog Butler (Hugh Millais), the leader of the zinc mine's hired assassins, is sitting in Sheehan's saloon getting the lay of things, he remarks that the railroaders figured out a way to dynamite tunnels by paying their Chinese laborers fifty dollars to set the dynamite off in the partly-dug tunnels. If it kills the coolie, that's one less Chinese; if he survives, it's money well spent.

The dominant feature of Presbyterian Church is the church for which it is named. The cleric, Mr. Elliott

(Corey Fischer), a dour, hell-breathing individual, preaches an end-of-the-world sermon over the grave of Bart Coyl, and takes McCabe's rifle when McCabe climbs the steeple to look for Butler and his cutthroats. He gives McCabe the excuse that rifles have no place in a house of God. Butler, in his search for McCabe, comes upon Elliott with the rifle, shoots his arm off, and inadvertently starts the fire in the church. This creates a diversion that distracts the townsfolk from paying attention to McCabe's plight as he battles Butler, Breed (Jace Vander Veen), and the Kid (Manfred Shulz) in the snow.

A man carrying the cross on his back is silhouetted against the setting sun (the first time we see the church and its spire) as he completes the steeple while McCabe brings his first consignment of prostitutes back from Bear Paw. The whores become a part of the social life (in fact they *are* the social life) of Presbyterian Church to such an extent that they, too, help put out the fire at the church and share in the celebratory bottle which is passed around after it's extinguished. They are accepted with the same casual attitude as the Kid's wanton shooting of the Cowboy (Keith Carradine). As the Kid challenges the Cowboy, who is crossing the rope bridge, Sheehan, Breed, and Dog Butler stand looking at the activity with little more than passing curiosity. They think it's pointless, but they aren't about to interfere.

Biology plays an important role in the life of Presbyterian Church. One of McCabe's whores, living in a tent, empties a bucket of slops into the road; one of Mrs. Miller's conditions for setting up McCabe's house is that there will be a proper bathhouse for the men and hygiene will be attended to so there will be no danger of infection. Eugene Sears (Michael Murphy) worries over the meat as he and his partner prepare to leave the town, having failed

Julie Christie operates an opium kit

to do business with McCabe, and Sears remarks, "All I need now is a case of the runs."

One of Altman's most important collaborations has been the ongoing one with Leon Ericksen. Ericksen has been responsible for the look of Altman's films from *M*A*S*H* on, with the exception of *Thieves Like Us*. He and Altman studied photos of the West at the turn of the century. Altman explains: "We try to get a certain kind of antiquity look to it that would be sort of reminiscent. We had the color control. Nobody could walk in with a red sweater unless we wanted them to. To get the mood or the feeling, we tried to go for the reality of what kind of light there would have been then. We were dealing with gas or oil lanterns all the time, and we tried to use that color and match that kind of light. We prefogged the film to get just a little antique effect on it. We did an awful lot of tests. We were shooting a scene with Julie Christie on the bridge and it started to snow. Big flakes. I said, 'Let's get this real quick,' and we shot it. You're so used to that weather up there . . . then suddenly it starts feeling really cold about ten o'clock at night and I had Marcel Vercoutere, who was our special-effects guy and ran the rain, I said, 'Go see what the temperature is.' It was thirty-one. I said, 'Let's freeze it.' So we stayed up all night and we turned the hoses and rain on and we just froze that. [Warren Beatty asked him how long it would take to shoot and said,] 'The snow doesn't last up here.' I said, 'Well, we haven't anything else to do.' So with a little bit of reluctance we started filming, and it literally didn't stop for eight days. I mean it was up to here. The only problem was that we had to overlay some falling snow optically because sometimes we had it and sometimes we didn't. That's what made it a movie."

Michael Murphy recalls aspects of shooting *McCabe*

and Mrs. Miller with Altman: "Warren likes to do a lot of takes, so he would do a lot of takes for him. He was fine on the third take. And then Julie, she's great right off the bat, so he had to work both ways, and shoot few takes with her and more with Warren. It was good for the picture, it was good for Warren."

Like the rest of Altman's films, *McCabe and Mrs. Miller* is concerned with people who are trying to make their way in a world with which they are, in some important respects, out of tune. McCabe isn't smart enough to see that when big business wants your small business, you don't argue, you settle up and leave. Mrs. Miller, of course, tunes out literally. It's too easy to see her as society's victim, the woman who has raised herself a step above being merely a prostitute, but who will now, with her partner gone, be forced to slide back into total degradation. As Cohen's song says, "You chose your journey long before you came upon this highway."

The other Cohen song Altman uses in the film is "Sisters of Mercy," which describes the whores in glowing and loving terms. To some degree Altman sentimentalizes these girls in much the same way Cohen's song does, and just as falsely. The girls are portrayed as chummy girl-scout types who care about and for each other. One scene shows them brushing each other's hair; another depicts a birthday party with a cake and candles and squeals of delight for the plump blonde who blows out all the candles. Even under the iron-spined tutelage of a Mrs. Miller, it's hard to believe that such camaraderie would be likely.

McCabe and Mrs. Miller is the most satisfying of Altman's films to see and contemplate. It is physically beautiful, it has marvelous performances, and is realistic about situations and characters who are all too easy to sentimentalize. Altman almost does become syrupy about them, but restrains himself in time, usually cutting to a contrasting action that puts everything into perspective. The film has none of the annoying cuteness that occasionally mars movies like *M*A*S*H* and *The Long Goodbye*, and none of the deliberate archness that detracts from the potential both *Brewster McCloud* and *Images* at first seem to offer. As Pauline Kael states: "*McCabe and Mrs. Miller* seems so strange because, despite a great deal of noise about the art of film, we are unaccustomed to an intuitive, quixotic, essentially impractical approach to moviemaking, and to an exploratory approach to a subject, particularly when the subject is the American past. A movie like this isn't made by winging it; to improvise in a period setting takes phenomenal discipline, but *McCabe and Mrs. Miller* doesn't look 'disciplined,' as movies that lay everything out for the audience do."

Images

Images is a film about a woman who may or may not be going mad, who may or may not have killed her lovers and her husband, but who is certainly in the process of writing a book called *In Search of Unicorns*, about some Tolkien-like elves and sprites, and who has a young friend, the daughter of one of the lovers, who resembles her very closely. This is all the "plot" the film has; *Images* is a consideration of a woman at a time in her life when she seems to be trying to find herself through writing. It has very much the same feeling of reverie that *3 Women* does, and more than a few echoes of that other famous film about a blonde young lady going mad, *Repulsion*. Altman could have "dreamed" *Images* as he did *3 Women*; it has the same properties of being both the product of a lucid, organized mind and of a fevered dream by someone who has been reading too much Lawrence Durrell.

Unfortunately, Altman has marred what might have been a sensitive study of a certain kind of schizophrenia with some lazy and labored effects that have the result of making one want to write the whole film off as an interesting try that failed because of insufficient thought. For example, Cathryn is played by Susannah York and Susannah is played by Cathryn Harrison. Hugh is played by René Auberjonois, René is played by Marcel Bozzuffi,

René Auberjonois on IMAGES

and Hugh Millais plays Marcel, a labored conceit if ever there was one. Stomu Yamash'ta, who gets credit for the "sounds," does a lot of fiddling with electronic noises, sighs, and the wind chimes that Cathryn has hung everywhere, but instead of commenting on what is happening, the noises interfere with one's concentration. *Images* is a film that should be seen stoned, or with every pore open and alert to catch each nuance. The sounds get in the way of the nuances. Certainly one reacts emotionally, as Altman keeps saying he wants his audiences to, to what he has put on the screen, not so much to Cathryn's torment, but to the murders, which are gory and explicit.

Although the film was made in Ireland, in a particularly gorgeous stretch of country, the filmmakers seem to want the audience to believe that it is laid in the United States, even though all the actors except

Marcel Bozzuffi as Rene

Auberjonois are continental. The phones that plague Cathryn in the opening are American, but the cars are British and drive on the left side of the road. The apartment block where Hugh and Cathryn live looks American-luxurious, but the station Hugh takes a train back to town from is European. If Altman's intention is to dislocate us geographically so we will concentrate on the action and the psychology of his heroine, he has succeeded only with his first aim.

Cathryn is beginning to fall apart at the seams even before she and Hugh take off for their country home. Hugh calls to say he's working late and a mysterious female voice, sounding suspiciously like Cathryn's own, keeps calling to tell her that he's having an affair. When Hugh returns, he changes before her eyes into the image of her dead lover, René. Cathryn goes berserk and Hugh comforts her. Cathryn likes the peace of the country; Hugh likes to shoot quail with his rifle, and still lifes of deer heads and leaves with his camera, so they spend their time following their respective pleasures. During their stay, René turns up and plagues Cathryn, who shoots him, but he won't stay dead. Marcel, who apparently lusts after Cathryn, arrives with his young daughter, Susannah, who looks the way Cathryn must have when she was young. Marcel lumbers around the house after Cathryn, so she shoots him too, but he turns up alive not much later. She sees "herself" by the side of the road and shoves this self down a waterfall with her car, then drives back into town, where the "self," in an obvious echo of the *Psycho* shower scene, informs her that she really tossed Hugh down the waterfall. The film ends on a close-up of a

(previous page) Cathryn Harrison confronts Susannah York

Hugh Millais and Susannah York

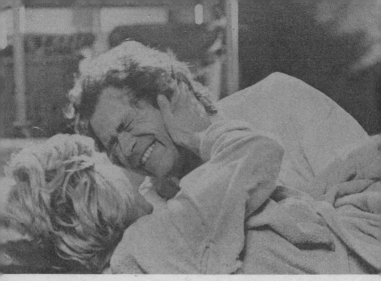

Susannah York and Hugh Millais

completed puzzle, which Susannah and Cathryn had been working on, showing the house, a unicorn, and a lion in a dark, nighttime setting.

Altman describes how *Images* came about: "I've worked on *Images* for six and a half years. I had this idea. I thought about it, and when I was in London, I started writing in my hotel room. Back in Los Angeles, I locked myself up in my office in Westwood, sent out for meals, and finished it." He decided on Susannah York after seeing her in *Jane Eyre* with George C. Scott. The house where most of the film takes place is near Dublin, "a white two-story house, set on a road between a lake and a mountain, forests around it and a waterfall, all so beautiful. . . ." Altman further commented, "Some will reject [*Images*] because they won't understand the woman's lapses into madness; others will accept it, understanding that she is driven by fear and guilt."

But fear and guilt over what? Fear that Hugh may be having an affair? Guilt because she didn't want a child, according to René, and may or may not have been pregnant by him? Neither Cathryn's behavior nor Altman's script does more than allude to the causes for her dramatic attacks of schizophrenia. Very much the same sorts of problems arise in *Images* as did in *Brewster McCloud*, and they stem from a central shapelessness, an almost unwieldy resistance to being dealt with on such a concrete level as film. *Brewster* wants to be a narrative poem and *Images* wants to be written by Sylvia Plath. It seems that this has less to do with the idea of having a narrative drive, or alternatively, of being a series of sketches which revolve around the figure of Cathryn, who just happens to be driving herself insane, than it does with the lack of a nucleus for the figures to revolve around. Everything in *Repulsion* referred to or stemmed from Carol's madness, but the men and the young girl in *Images* have lives and volitions of their own. They intrude on Cathryn when she's not prepared for them, and she's so

Reality vs. imagination: Auberjonois, York, and Millais

emotionally defenseless that she has no mechanisms for dealing with them except to try to literally murder them. Since it's impossible to kill a figment of one's imagination, it's hardly surprising that she doesn't succeed, and a film about someone failing to perform an impossible task would have to be made more carefully than *Images* was, to succeed.

Altman later got onto surer ground in this area and was able to make the nonheroes of *California Split* and the foolish hero figure of *Buffalo Bill and the Indians* into individuals of charm, pathos, and considerable interest. For all of his empathy for and appreciation of women, Altman consistently (that is, until *3 Women*) does better by his men.

Images is also unnecessarily tricky cinematically. The wind chimes dance around the foregrounds of many shots, there is an impossible infinity of mirrors, baubles, reflecting camera lenses, eyeballs. Vilmos Zsigmond has filled the screen with beautiful, lucid images that have as little meaning as the film itself. Altman has made a film that's impossible to like—it's cold to the point of freezing in spite of the warm Irish scenery—and impossible to ignore. No one could want to lift it out of the Altman canon and pretend it never happened, but it's embarrassing. Hugh and Cathryn have such a loveless relationship that one feels as though one is intruding on something painful when they simply talk to each other. Is she frigid? Is that why, despite the sterility of her marriage, she refuses to have sex with Marcel when he chases her around? What is the purpose, to the viewers, of Cathryn's book, *In Search of Unicorns* (which Susannah York did, in fact, write)? Are we supposed to feel that because she can write a book for children, she must love and want her own? Or is the book an excuse for not

Susannah York

having children or an apology to unborn infants for not bearing them? (Ironically, Susannah York was pregnant when she flimed *Images*. Her figure is beginning to fill out, and she hardly looks as strained and harried as a lady in her predicament might. She looks in the pink of health.)

Images played in the tenth New York Film Festival and in the 1972 Filmex, the Los Angeles film festival. It opened to disappointing reviews, among which is Andrew Sarris's *Village Voice* criticism: "Even the pattern of mystification seems trivially complicated rather than truly complex. All that is hoped for from the implications of the images evaporates with the clearing up of the foggy plot. And so the movie 'means' nothing, or at most, very little." *Images* went down in ignominious defeat, its death at the box office attributable to similar critical slaughter.

Images is a difficult film which unfortunately creates no interest in coming to grips with those difficulties, as other Altman films do. *The Long Goodbye*, Altman's next film, is also "difficult," but the problems are worth surmounting and the pleasures therein are many.

The Long Goodbye

"It is not funny that a man should be killed, but it is sometimes funny that he should be killed for so little, and that his death should be the coin of what we call civilization.... But down these mean streets a man must go who is not himself mean, who is neither tarnished nor afraid. The detective in this kind of story must be such a man. He is the hero; he is everything. He must be a complete man and a common man and yet an unusual man. He must be, to use a rather weathered phrase, a man of honor—by instinct, by inevitability, without thought of it, and certainly without saying it. He must be the best man in the world and a good enough man for any world. I do not care much about his private life; he is neither a eunuch nor a satyr; I think he might seduce a duchess and I am quite sure he would not spoil a virgin; if he is a man of honor in one thing, he is that in all things.

"He is a relatively poor man, or he would not be a detective at all. He will take no man's money dishonestly and no man's insolence without a due and dispasssionate revenge. He is a lonely man and his pride is that you will treat him as a proud man or be very sorry you ever saw him. He talks as the man of his age talks—that is, with rude wit, a lively sense of the grotesque, a disgust for sham, and a contempt for pettiness. He has a range of

awareness that startles you, but it belongs to him by right, because it belongs to the world he lives in. If there were enough like him, the world would be a very safe place to live in, without becoming too dull to be worth living in."
—"The Simple Art of Murder," an essay by Raymond Chandler

When it was released in 1973, *The Long Goodbye* drew fire from several critics and those of its audience who were diehard Raymond Chandler fans for not being faithful to the plot and, in some respects, to the mores of the original, which was, after all, written in 1953. Altman and his writer, Leigh Brackett, who had worked on the 1946 film version of Chandler's *The Big Sleep*, updated the action to the seventies and, at the suggestion of Brian Hutton, who was briefly involved with the project, drastically changed the ending.

Altman spoke to an interviewer about what he had done: "The research material we used primarily was *Raymond Chandler Speaking*, a series of letters, and I made everybody that worked on the picture read that thoroughly. I took the two characters, both Philip Marlowe and Roger Wade, and I took character traits of Chandler and I applied them to both, and I made one the voice and one the conscience. His plots are so complicated and so full of holes that the way he plugged the holes was to further complicate them. But he used this thread to hang about sixty thumbnail essays on, so the real interest in Raymond Chandler, to me, were those essays. We tightened the plot up; I dropped half the characters, probably; then I used that line to hang a bunch of film essays on. They weren't actually lifted from Raymond Chandler as much as they were my projection of him, because if Raymond Chandler were alive in 1972 he

Elliott Gould as Philip Marlowe in THE LONG GOODBYE

wouldn't see things the way he did in 1950 [*sic*] because he would himself have been that much older. I've kept the story in 1952, but set it in 1972. The goodbye is people going, not in separate directions, but going in the same direction at a different pace."

The film's plot concerns Marlowe's (Elliott Gould) friendship wiht Terry Lennox (Jim Bouton), who turns up óne night with scratches on his hands and face and asks Marlowe to drive him to Mexico. He explains that he had a nasty fight with his wife, Sylvia; in fact Sylvia has been murdered. Marlowe is detained in jail because of his involvement with Terry. A call from Eileen Wade (Nina van Pallandt) sends Marlowe in search of her husband, Roger Wade (Sterling Hayden), a writer with severe emotional problems who's drying out in a suspicious clinic run by a Dr. Verringer (Henry Gibson). Marlowe receives a note from Lennox containing a "Madison" (a five-thousand-dollar bill) and a note saying he's sorry and goodbye. This and the last developments in the plot constitute the titular "long goodbye." Marty Augustine (Mark Rydell) and his thugs visit Marlowe, claiming that Lennox was carrying $355,000 for him, and since Marlowe was the last person to see Lennox alive (he has committed suicide in Mexico, according to the papers), Marlowe presumably knows where the money is. Marlowe tails Augustine to the Wade house, discovering an apparent connection between the Wades and Lennoxes, who live in the same beach colony, and Augustine. After a party at the Wade home, where Roger Wade is accosted by Dr. Verringer, who demands and is paid some money, Roger sleeps off his liquor, then wanders into the sea. The police who arrive to investigate Wade's suicide reveal that Wade, who had been having an affair with Sylvia Lennox, went directly from her home, the afternoon she was killed, to Verringer's rest home. Eileen was afraid that Roger had killed Sylvia in a jealous rage and then forgotten about it. Augustine threatens Marlowe unless he turns the money over, but is interrupted. As Marlowe departs, he spots a bag full of cash. Leaving Augustine's building, he sees Eileen driving away. Marlowe journeys to Mexico, where he "donates" the five-thousand-dollar bill to the police coroner for information. The trail leads him to Lennox, safely tucked away in a sylvan hideaway. Lennox confesses that he killed Sylvia, that he had been sleeping with Eileen and was worried over being Augustine's courier. His faked suicide solved his problems and now Eileen, who has more money than Sylvia and Augustine together, is on her way to him. Marlowe pulls a pistol out and shoots the surprised Lennox, who drops into the nearby stream still holding his drink. As Marlowe walks away, Eileen passes him driving a jeep.

Those who were outraged at the liberties Altman took with Chandler's plot were most upset by the ending. Leigh Brackett recalls that Brian Hutton didn't like her suggestion "and said, 'I'd rather see Marlowe kill the guy.' I thought, 'That sounds pretty good, let's do it that way.' The original ending, the one in the novel, was pretty inconclusive and didn't please any of us, so we thought we'd go for broke and see what happened."

Altman tells the story of the woman who spoke to him after a screening of the film. She had a worried expression and asked the director, "Isn't he going to get in trouble for that?" She was serious; she was thinking in terms of the other Chandler or Dashiell Hammett detective films, in which that sort of behavior had its just and logical retribution.

Altman talked to Paul Gardner of the *New York Times*

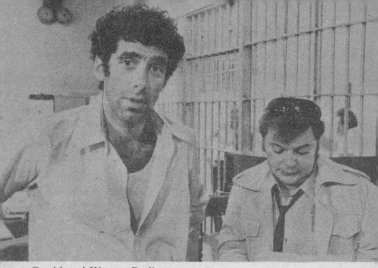

Gould and Warren Berlinger

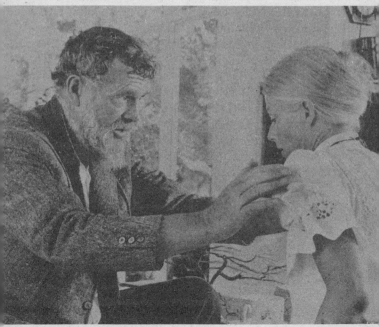

Sterling Hayden and Nina van Pallandt

in November 1973, after the film had opened a second time in New York: "Many people still won't like it because television and pop novels have conditioned us to endings with moral justice. My detective has a preconceived idea about morality, and he's wrong. He foolishly enters a case emotionally, based on friendship. He ends it with gunfire. Audiences are disturbed because it raises questions about their own moral hypocrisy."

United Artists was disturbed, too, when the film opened and fell through the floor. They did what few other distributors would be inclined to do. They took the film out of circulation, thought about it for a while (they thought about changing the title, about shortening it, and about reediting it) and then reopened the movie with a new ad campaign by *Mad* magazine artist Jack Davis, which sold Philip Marlowe as a quirky, sloppy "new" detective with a cat. The film did very well in New York, but not at all well around the country, where it had opened earlier with the original ads. The film did make the *New York Times* Ten Best list, and Vilmos Zsigmond won the National Society of Film Critics' award as best cinematographer for his work on the film.

Altman's point about Chandler's plot not being as important as his character analyses serves as a convenient point of view from which he could act with his customary lack of concern for the plot of this particular work. Both Chandler and Altman are always interested in character, how it influences behavior, and the interaction of certain types of behavior under specific conditions. Some of the dialogue clearly belongs neither to Chandler, Brackett, nor Altman, but to the actor who improvised it. This is true of many of Sterling Hayden's lines, and of some of Gould's Marlowe dialogue, much of which has the same rhythm and form as his dialogue in *M* A* S* H*, *namely*

Gould and John Davey

when he talks to himself. But Marlowe talks to himself not because he's a supercool hipster, but because he's alone; not necessarily lonely, but solitary, without friends. He rambles through the film looking shaggy, shabby, and carrying on a running monologue with himself about whatever's on his mind or in front of his eyes. When he loses his cat, Marlowe asks the spaced-out, seminude girls next door to keep an eye out for it. They answer through a drugged haze, and Marlowe comments that they aren't even there. Returning from the supermarket, where he has been unable to find the cat's favorite Curry brand food, he puts the food from a new can into an old Curry tin, mumbling as he labors, "I love the cat, I love the cat." He tried to fool the (nameless) animal, the offering is rejected, and the cat exits through a hole in a window, labeled "El Porto del Gato," presumably to look for better fare elsewhere. Many reviewers leaped on this sequence as being emblematic of the "new" Marlowe. The old one didn't have a cat, didn't talk to himself, and wasn't a walking shambles. Throughout the film this Philip Marlowe wears the same crumpled black suit, J. C. Penney tie, and clean white shirt, and is either clean-shaven or sports a heavy five-o'clock shadow.

But there are holdovers from Chandler's Marlowe: The apartment, while not exactly the sort of place his detective would live in, is of the forties-fifties vintage, California stucco with a creaky, cranky elevator—more the kind of place the book's Marlowe had his office in. Altman's Marlowe has no office; he operates out of his flat and a bar where he collects phone messages. He has a 1948 Lincoln Continental, highly polished and obviously maintained with loving care. The car is the tangible symbol of the literary Marlowe hidden within his 1973 incarnation. (In 1975 Dick Richards made *Farewell, My*

Lovely, also with changes and starring Robert Mitchum, looking the part but around twenty years too old for it, as Philip Marlowe.) Elliott Gould's Marlowe is in the *mode* of the Humphrey Bogart, Dick Powell Marlowes. With a few modifications, they have the same code of ethics. Bogart's Marlowe wouldn't have killed Terry Lennox, but then no film Bogart appeared in would have given him a script calling for the kind of action Gould gets involved in. Powell's Marlowe might have killed; he had a shorter temper and, although he possessed a sense of irony, he had little ironic *distance* from the exertions he was caught up in. Mitchum's Marlowe is something of a sentimental dope. He's closer to the truth than the cops, but he acts as a catalyst for actions that take place around him rather than directly influencing them. Gould's Marlowe has irony but no distance; he's involved— because Lennox was his friend, because he was in a position of trust, and because he trusted someone he liked—and he makes things happen. He removes Wade from Dr. Verringer's clutches, but he's powerless to prevent Wade's suicide, or even to know right away why it should have been necessary. He's furious at the cops because they withheld information from him, even though he refused to give *them* information about Lennox. The "Madison" was intended either to buy Marlowe's silence or to pay him for the favor of driving Lennox to the Mexican border. Marlowe has a nice sense of justice, a tidy mind to contrast with his shapeless body, which demands that mysteries should be solved, that the legal and emotional books should be balanced. He exacts no revenge from Marty Augustine, because Augustine has been merely an inconvenience and besides, he's surrounded by hoods ready to grind Marlowe up, given the go-ahead. He yells at the cops for playing everything so close to the vest, but he really revenges himself on those who betrayed him, by killing Lennox and showing the police that he's discovered the "real truth." And he pays Eileen Wade back for lying to him. No wonder Marlowe, in a reprise with variations of the ending from *The Third Man*, plays his toy harmonica and dances in the road as he walks away from Lennox's body, passing a surprised Eileen, heading toward her now-dead lover.

Gould and Altman have made their Marlowe an idiosyncratic loner with a certain raffish charm and a cool mien that seems laid back but is, in fact, all wary attention and never misses a thing. It's his business to be suspicious, but never to show it without reason. As he and Eileen are eating dinner after the party at which Dr. Verringer extorted $4,600 (supposedly for fees, but really as hush money), he flatters her cooking, she tells him to call her Eileen, and he responds, "Okay, Eileen, what was Marty Augustine doing here the other night?" Eileen clams up and her face becomes closed, but Marlowe's on the trail of information and he won't stop till he has his curiosity satisfied.

Altman spoke about Gould's characterization and about how he got involved in the film while he was still working on it, in October of 1972: "He is fantastic. He is brilliant. He is the only Philip Marlowe. Jerry Bick and Elliott Kastner had acquired the rights to the thing and had made a deal with UA. They asked me if I'd be interested, and I said, 'No, I don't want to do that sort of thing.' David Picker had said he would accept Elliott Gould. Gould was blackballed by the studios after that Warner Brothers thing, *A Glimpse of Tiger*. He was uninsurable and couldn't get a job. They just determined that Elliott was emotionally unstable and collected their insurance money on it. He didn't work for a couple of

Mark Rydell (as Marty Augustine) with Gould

years. David Picker, who had great faith in Elliott, said, 'I want to go with him in this thing. I think he would be a good Philip Marlowe.' I said, 'I don't think anyone else can do it,' and I talked myself into telling Jerry why it was such a good idea. I convinced myself that I should make the picture."

This Marlowe is a chain-smoker who uses unfiltered (i.e., forties) cigarettes and wooden matches, which he strikes with casual abandon on whatever's handiest, unmindful of the marks the suphur makes. Typically, he enters a house or a room in the act of lighting up and strikes his match on the doorway, never looking at the match, but concentrating on what's going on in the room, flicking his match away into the middle distance. Marlowe concentrates on what's going on or coming up, not on his appearance, or even, seemingly, on how he comes across to people. Marlowe has a "stupid" act he does for the police and for Augustine, but it's a shuck. Everyone sees, if not through it, around it. It's only intended to buy time, not to avoid the inevitable.

Marlowe can be kind. He really cares for his cat and he's even nice to Harry (David Arkin), the incredibly stupid thug Augustine assigns to stick with him. He gives Harry "tailing" lessons and, in one of the funniest scenes, even writes down the Wades' address in case Harry gets lost in traffic. He tells Harry to be neat, and when they both arrive at their destination and Harry can't go into the Wades' yard, he leaps on the door, which swings open. Marlowe buys brownie mix for the spaced-out girls next door, and when Marlowe leaves for the Wades', he and Harry have a discussion about what those druggy ladies do for a living. Marlowe tells Harry they make candles and have a nice little shop downtown. Harry, with a certain petulance, replies, "I can remember when people just had jobs." Marlowe doesn't mind taking time with people as long as they don't distract him or get in his way. And he'll take all the time he needs if he thinks he'll learn something.

Altman and Brackett simplified the plot, and Marlowe's character, to the point where they dropped a few essential ingredients along the way. Marlowe has a much keener appreciation of women than his treatment, however admiring, of Eileen Wade would indicate. Time and again, in the books, he tosses willing women away like so many used matches. Once in a while he makes love to them, but only under the most scrupulously observed conditions—they can't be psychotics, he has to be fairly sure of their innocence in whatever case he's involved in, and he has to really like them.

Chandler's Marlowe is punctiliously neat; he's no lovable slob like Altman's, and in many ways it might have been more of a challenge if Altman had left that orderliness in, rather than falling back on quirky sloppiness and a cat. But basically Altman is faithful to the spirit, if not to the letter, of Chandler's creation.

The other focal point of the film is Terry Lennox, whose character is totally ignored until it comes time to reveal him as a louse. The book's Lennox was a far more ambiguous creation, and Marlowe, having discovered the truth about his friend, lets him go. Baseball player Jim Bouton does well by his first screen role in the brief time alotted to him. He makes one see the callous charm, the easy cynicism, and the amorality that was presumably disguised in his earlier friendship with Marlowe.

Nina van Pallandt is also effective in her American screen debut. She's warm, equivocating, and a crook, but she cares about her husband. Her face crumples in their long lacerating scene together, the morning after Marlowe has delivered Wade from the clutches of Dr. Verringer. She's an instinctive rather than a trained actress, and Altman uses this aspect of her screen persona the way he uses the same quality in Shelley Duvall. He lets them play characters not too far removed from themselves, individuals who don't have such a wide range of emotions to portray that they'll be forced to depict behavior they aren't familiar with. Van Pallandt is good as the wily seductress who tries to tame her unstable and unruly husband and who flirts with Marlowe to keep him guessing, but who, all the time this double and even triple game was going on, is the mistress of Lennox, safely stashed across the border waiting for her arrival so they can share her money and his anonymity in style.

The third fascinating portrayal is that of Sterling Hayden's Roger Wade, the blocked writer who needs to dry out in suspicious clinical way-stations, and who's been carrying on a lengthy affair with Lennox's vixen wife, Sylvia. Hayden comes dangerously close to self-parody. He looks like Jack D. Ripper from *Dr. Strangelove* playing Captain Ahab in *Moby Dick*. He's spaced out and clumsy, but with an underlying aura of sarcasm that's a clue to the reality of the foxy grandpa beneath the "grand old drunk by the sea," act he's doing for those who aren't wise to him. Hayden does so much "shtick" that it's hard to tell if there's much of Hayden beneath it all. If Altman goes for "behaviors," rather than actors, as he's said, he certainly got his money's worth when he hired Hayden. Hayden liked his role and professed great admiration for Altman. He said, "This is my last movie role. I'm going out on this one. It'll be the only role I'm not ashamed of. I'm going to let it all out. All of it. It's easy because the role of Roger Wade is so close to myself. A man who drinks because he's afraid of fear and failure, afraid he may be a coward." Actually, Hayden's behavior is like a bluff version of his role in *The Killing*, a film he made for Stanley Kubrick in 1956. Altman's simplification has the effect of obscuring the reasons for Roger Wade's behavior. In the book Wade is murdered—the death is faked to look like suicide—and his actions are explained in several of the thumbnail essays Altman is so fond of. Here, no one knows why he commits suicide—is it because he feels guilty about his affair with Sylvia, and/or because he's afraid he killed her and can't remember? He makes a mysterious allusion to Augustine owing *him* money. Is he broke? Or is he fearful that he's lost both his wife's love and his gift for writing? Virtually any combination of the above would be enough to send a lot of people into the sea. But not saying exactly why Wade killed himself has the effect of adding mystery to mystery when the first was quite sufficiently confusing.

Hayden has several good scenes, the first of which takes place the morning after Wade has been returned to Eileen. Marlowe stops by to see how they're getting along and Hayden attacks her with a sarcastic early morning toast, "To us." She makes a dig about his virility and soon they're going at each other, but with such an undercurrent of sadness that it's like a love scene scored for shrieks rather than for soft, cooing sounds. It's pathetic and believable; it comes from the lexicon of recognizable human behavior. *We all*, Altman seems to be saying, could play this scene. It's small, human-scaled, like *Brief Encounter*, and made more poignant by the posh surroundings of the Wades' beachfront luxury. Money can't buy happiness, lack of money buys misery, but that isn't the real problem bothering any of these people. Wade's guttural accusations, which sound like boozy philosophizing, are an attempt to get at the truth and to evade it at the same time. "Maybe, maybe, maybe, you've already left me," he tells Eileen, when she says she'll leave him if he doesn't quit drinking. He apologizes and holds her, she responds, but soon they're at it again, clearly entwined in a long-running stalemate. Wade sarcastically calls her "Contessa," an allusion to her refined British accent and her classic good looks, and to the fact that he comes by his affectations somewhat less naturally. He's changed his name; marrying Eileen was a step on the upwardly mobile social ladder. These many layers of details, accretions, emerge almost accidentally, but they're all to the point and all enormously indicative of character. They tell Marlowe, who's out of earshot, but in sight, a great deal about the people he's involved with.

The scenes with Marty Augustine are harder to define. The novel's Augustine, while a thug of the old school, was refined. This one is a Jewish hipster, with a star of David,

Hayden, Gould, van Pallandt, and Henry Gibson

an ethnically balanced entourage of hoods, and a mistress who gets a Coke bottle in the face so Augustine can prove to Marlowe what a tough guy he is. He's also sensitive to his thugs' needs. When one of them objects to stripping, because he has knife scars on his body, in an elaborate ritual Augustine proposes for discovering who's honest, Augustine lets him leave the room. Augustine is an adherent of the pop methodology of keeping everyone off balance, so that no one can get the better of him. He's a thoroughly detestable punk but, as is so often the case, a fascinating one.

The cops' motivations are considerably harder to decipher. They want to know why Lennox needed to be driven to Mexico just after his wife died, but they're not very curious about why Wade checked into Dr. Verringer's about the same time. They're more interested in rousting Marlowe about than in dealing with scum like Marty Augustine and Dr. Verringer, whose clinic is questionable, to say the least. Marlowe's anger at them, just after Wade's death, is completely justifiable, but he sounds like an irate individual trying to make a citizen's arrest, not like a hip detective whose client has just mysteriously decided to end his life. One can infer that his rage is a contributing factor to the avenging-angel stance he adopts when dispatching Lennox. Marlowe isn't mad just over the personal discomfort he's been caused; he's angry at Lennox's attitude that he had a right to carry on in this high-handed fashion.

The other innovation in *The Long Goodbye* is the John Williams–Johnny Mercer ballad, which is the movie's theme song. After the opening, "Hooray for Hollywood," which Altman uses to tell the audience that this is a movie (as he so frequently does, *M*A*S*H* and *Brewster McCloud* being the best examples) the music switches to the title ballad, which is sung over the credits. The theme music recurs in many guises, as a ballad, as a love theme, but recognizable as the same "long goodbye" that the raspy-voiced singer drawls about at the beginning. When Marlowe collects his phone messages at the bar, a piano player is noodling at the tune, it's under Marlowe's scrounging around his apartment looking for catfood, it's the Muzak at the supermarket, it's all over, but always the tune is subtly altered in style, so that it fits into the context it's used in.

Altman has said that he used constant camera movement in *The Long Goodbye* to draw the viewer into the film. The panning is not random, nor as casual as the director implies it is. The eye is drawn away from one area to another to make visual points. Altman begins the film panning over the entry to Marlowe's apartment, past a

Elliott Gould and Nina van Pallandt

wall, and finds Marlowe asleep with his clothes on in bed.
His cat enters, and climbs around until Marlowe realizes
it's hungry. Marlowe stumbles up, talking to himself and
the cat, and tries to fool the animal with a homemade mess,
which the cat rejects by pawing it off the edge of the
kitchen counter. Altman has introduced the audience to
Marlowe, the tired working stiff, and to the fact that his
cat is important to him. The audience has seen Marlowe's

apartment and the visual technique Altman will employ throughout the film: the first-person camera. Nothing can be seen or known that Marlowe doesn't see or know. Chandler wrote the Marlowe novels in the first person, and the camera is Altman's instrument for maintaining the device. The one time Altman has to cheat on this method is during the argument between Roger and Eileen Wade. Marlowe tactfully withdraws to the beach "to count the waves," as he says, but his reflection is seen on the doors behind which the Wades alternately attack and comfort each other.

The sound for *The Long Goodbye* was handled by John V. Speak in a conventional mike-and-boom manner, but it sounds as though Lion's Gate 8-Track Sound was used. (*California Split* was the first film to use the eight-track system.) It isn't "pure"; there's room noise, overlapping dialogue, and at times a cacophony of sounds, at other times an almost artificial quiet, as when Marlowe arrives at night and searches Dr. Verringer's rest area for Wade.

The film is notable for its offbeat casting: Jim Bouton, who was a baseball player, author *(Ball Four)*, and sports commentator, Nina van Pallandt, Clifford Irving's ex-girlfriend; Henry Gibson, known principally as a comedian on television's *Laugh-In*; and Mark Rydell, an actor turned director who went back to directing immediately following *The Long Goodbye*, taking Altman's cameraman, Vilmos Zsigmond, and his art director, Leon Ericksen, with him to work on *Cinderella Liberty*.

Thieves Like Us

Robert Altman's tenth film, *Thieves Like Us*, is one of his most successful on many levels—except at the box office, where it died an untimely, and apparently premature death. That small segment of the audience for any film which went to *Thieves Like Us* seemingly remembers it with affection, but, perhaps in remembrance of its first ignominious failure, it is seldom revived today. As Altman says, "The best reviews I've ever had, across the board, were on *Thieves Like Us*. You could shoot a shotgun off. That's the place they ought to practice bombing. The critics are important. I wouldn't be making films if there were no critics. If I went strictly on my commercial record, I would not be working."

The film derives from Edward Anderson's 1937 novel of the same title, which was the source for Nicholas Ray's 1949 movie *They Live by Night*, which starred Farley Granger and Cathy O'Donnell as Bowie and Keechie, and Howard da Silva as Chickamaw. There are fundamental differences in Ray's and Altman's conceptions: Ray locates his film in the forties, when it was made. Altman's is located in the thirties, nearly forty years ago, and is made in color, whereas Ray's is the black-and-white of *noir* imagery. Granger and O'Donnell are more romantic figures than the Bowie and Keechie of Keith Carradine and Shelley Duvall. Where *They Live by Night* uses the song "I Know Where I'm Going" as an ironic commentary on the directionless lives Granger and O'Donnell are forced to live, Altman uses old radio programs as thematic counterpoint and a sort of second narrative for his film (there is no music score). But neither the similarities nor the differences really matter, for Altman has created a completely original film, one that bears comparison with the best of his work, and with many of the best hunted-criminals films of all time: *The Desperate Hours*, *Bonnie and Clyde*, *Little Caesar*, *The Killers*, *Dead End*, *The Roaring Twenties*, *White Heat*, and so on.

The film opens in the white mist of a Mississippi dawn as Bowie and Chickamaw, having escaped the state prison, meet up with T-Dub (Bert Remsen), who brings them a change of clothes in a taxi driven by a fat, scared driver they call "Jasbo." They hole up first with Dee Mobley (Tom Skerritt) and Keechie in Dee's rundown service station, then with Mattie (Louise Fletcher) and her children, who live with Mattie's sister Lula (Ann Latham), a dyed blonde whose black roots always show in spite of the fact that she's studying to be a beautician, and who drives T-Dub mad with desire. Mattie's husband is in jail himself; the only man who isn't imprisoned is Dee, and he complains that he never had his name in the paper, as if envying the notoriety and danger that being a bank robber provides the other men. The film is then alternately concerned with the ill-planned and reckless robberies the men commit, their wanton self-destructiveness, and the burgeoning romance between the two innocents, Keechie and Bowie.

This romance begins when the three men (or more accurately two men and a boy) stay at Dee's, and Bowie and Keechie hang around on the porch together drinking

Bert Remsen, John Schuck, and Keith Carradine in
THIEVES LIKE US

Coke and listening to the radio. Bowie makes vulgar and not too successful jokes for his own and Keechie's amusement, usually having to do with the state of Mississippi: "What's the state tree? A telephone pole." "What's the state animal? A squashed dog in the road." It's an awkward courtship carried out by two innocent, rawboned and likable country kids who learn, through their need for each other, how to express affection and, virtually for the first time, how to have fun with another person. But, aside from the problems presented by Bowie's being constantly on the lam, the young people are constrained by their lack of knowledge of the world at large and their virtually unconquerable naïveté.

The script Calder Willingham was commissioned to write by producer Jerry Bick, and which was rewritten by

Joan Tewkesbury and Altman after Altman came into the production, shows this hesitant flirtation as a series of shy smiles and halting conversations between the gawky acquaintances. Keechie's ears peek through her lank hair as she reaches for her cigarettes in her shapeless sweater and allows that she has never had a boyfriend, not even to walk her to church. Keechie's attitude is one of dispirited acceptance of her lot. She has little to look back on or forward to, and the presence of the gentle boy engaged in a romantic life of crime brings unexpected interest to her constricted existence.

But there is a basic, and supremely important, difference between Keechie and Bowie, whatever raw-boned, rural similarities they may share. Keechie is a survivor and Bowie isn't, not only because of the societal onus placed upon Bowie as being outside the law, but because Altman conceives of Keechie as being less vulnerable and chooses not to have her die with Bowie the way the novel has it. For all her gangling ineptitude and virginal inexperience, which masks an inner grace and self-possession, Keechie is made of fairly stern stuff. She rails at Bowie when he returns to their hideout cabin in the woods because he's pulled another job and she wanted him to quit. Such were her instincts for self-preservation that she's packed her bag, planning to leave after telling Bowie off, but, as Keechie says, "I don't want to leave ya." She had hoped he would have made her stay.

The change in their relationship from friends to lovers occurs as a result of an accident that takes place on the road while Bowie and Chicamaw are fooling around in their two cars on the way to Hermanville. Bowie crashes into a car at an intersection, and Chicamaw shoots two officers who try to prevent him from departing the scene with the injured Bowie. Chicamaw leaves Bowie with Dee and Keechie, and Dee abandons the two, not wishing to compromise his own position. Keechie stoically tells Bowie, whose face and chest are covered in blood, "You look awful," and uses the tail of her drooping sweater to wash his face. They set up housekeeping in Dee's ramshackle barn, Bowie on a pile of mattresses propped against a wall papered with sheet music from World War I, Keechie cooking on a wood stove and tending him by lantern light. Bowie has brought Keechie a watch, and Keechie covers Bowie with her one family heirloom, a patchwork quilt, in what is almost an exchange of gifts representing present and past. While the radio, tuned to a soupy version of *Romeo and Juliet*, intones, "Thus did Romeo and Juliet consummate their first interview by falling madly in love with each other," Keechie and Bowie kiss each other tentatively and begin to make love. (In an interview made at the time *Thieves Like Us* was released, Keith Carradine and Shelley Duvall commented on what Altman did with this scene. Carradine: "When we were doing it we weren't aware that it was being played for laughs. We were aware of the naïveté, of the awkwardness of the love scene, because these are two very young people in a very naïve period. That was all we knew we were doing. Of course, when it was cut together, you can see the awkwardness, and then throwing *Romeo and Juliet* over it shows you the humor. It's a paradoxical little thing that he does there." Duvall: "Keechie'd never had a boyfriend before in her life, so you can imagine the first time, it's going to be a lot awkward." Carradine: "When you sit back and look at it, especially with that thrown in there, all of a sudden you realize how funny it is. The awkwardness of it is amusing.") It's typical of their characters that neither one knows anything about sex except old wives' tales, which Keechie parrots and Bowie pooh-poohs, asking hopefully, "Do you want to do it again?" In spite of their lack of sophistication, they take to their new relationship readily, Keechie nonchalantly blowing smoke rings in bed, Bowie calling Keechie, "Honey," and the two of them making bird noises at each other and laughing. It's the first time either has cared for another person, and they show it with a special attentiveness and consideration, which for Bowie means telling Keechie, "I'm pretty deep in this business." He's warning her that he's seriously involved in a life of crime and has even killed some "laws," a boastful lie, since we know that the only murder he's committed is the one that resulted in his earlier incarceration.

While Bowie is recuperating at their lovers' hideaway, a cabin set in the middle of a forest, he plays catch with a local boy on the grass as Keechie watches. Although Bowie has said, "My only regret is that I never pitched pro ball," and she's encouraged him to think maybe he could, we're meant to see this as symbolic of his yearning for a straight life with normal values. But Bowie's resolve to quit the gang in response to Keechie's pleas are only halfhearted. He *is* "deep in this business," and lacks the intelligence and, truly, the will to get out of it. Bowie, like Chicamaw and T-Dub, is a drifter who meandered into robbery for lack of a better, or legitimate, occupation. Altman never invokes the Depression as a cause for the thieves' behavior, leaving the audience to conclude that they prefer this vocation, with its quick riches and its link, via radio and the press, to glamor.

Indeed, Altman means the three men to be seen as rootless, doomed strays, a notion enforced by the scene in which Bowie, temporarily separated from his cohorts, spends a night huddled under a railroad crossing, clutching a dog to him for warmth. Talking to himself for

Keith Carradine and Shelley Duvall in THIEVES LIKE US

companionship, Bowie asks the dog if he has a home or "Are you a thief like me?" Thief, to Bowie, means wanderer, and Altman intends the audience to see the men as being cut adrift from society, defeated at the outset by their own indifference to their fate, their self-destructive impulses and even by their loyalty to one another.

Altman conceives of Bowie and Keechie not as Bonnie and Clyde or any other romantic, on-the-lam couple, but as a pair of originals; neither as society's misfits nor as its elusive, crooked darlings. They are unique and, at the same time, typical of every misguided twosome, on either side of the law, ever created by fiction or real life. And it was Altman's genius to cast Keith Carradine and Shelley Duvall, two performers of unconventional (movie) appearance, as the ill-fated lovers. With their look of being permanently leggy, gauche adolescents, their prominent teeth and gawky/graceful movements, Carradine and Duvall are virtually typecast as the antithesis of Faye Dunaway and Warren Beatty, 1967's Bonnie Parker and Clyde Barrow.

Bowie, with his nasal twang, his repeated dumb jokes and wide, affecting grin, is a natural charmer, but his death at the end is felt, not as a loss on the part of the viewer, but as Keechie's loss. Keechie, sick and unwittingly pregnant, leaves her cabin at the Grapes Motel to visit Mattie while Bowie is away rescuing Chicamaw from the state pen. Bowie returns, entering the cabin (the unlucky Number 13 to which Mattie assigned them), and as the hidden troopers emerge from their ambush, Keechie starts toward Bowie. Altman focusses on her reaction as she stands at daybreak on Mattie's porch. Mattie holds Keechie by the shoulders to keep her from running to Bowie in their cabin, as the police pour bullets into it. Altman uses slow motion briefly (as he had in *McCabe* to show the death of the young cowboy, played coincidentally by Keith Carradine, as he crashed into a frozen river) to elaborate on Keechie's anguished response to Bowie's harrowing extinction. The troopers carry Bowie out, wrapped in Keechie's blood-soaked quilt, as the camera zooms in on one of Bowie's bullet-ripped shoes, stained with blood, as if to both particularize it as *Bowie's* shoe, belonging to someone we've come to like during the course of the film, and to establish an emotional distance from Bowie's corpse, that of someone who is, after all, just another punk with a gun.

That emotional distance is emphasized by the next scene, in which Keechie, waiting for a train to take her anywhere as long as it's away from her past, lies to the lady she's sitting next to (played by the co-scenarist, Joan Tewksesbury). She tells the woman about her husband, the father of the baby she's carrying, and that she won't name her child after him—"I think it'll be a boy"—because "he crossed me up once too often, lyin'"—a reference to Bowie's unfelt, and unkept, promises to quit the gang. Denying the circumstances of Bowie's death, she says he died of consumption. Keechie's disinterest in her destination is related to the gang's heedlessness in regard to its own fate. Keechie may be a survivor, but she's an uncaring one, and her callousness toward the memory of Bowie serves to remove her as an object of audience sympathy and also to remove some of her essential humanity as it was established in previous scenes. Altman isolates her even more by repeating the use of slow motion as Keechie, with her ever-present bottle of Coke, moves with the crowd up the stairs to the train.

Altman was as fortunate in his casting of Bowie's sidekicks, Chicamaw and T-Dub, as he was in having Carradine play Bowie. Both John Schuck and Bert Remsen had worked for Altman before. Schuck played the Painless Pole in *M*A*S*H*, the dumb cop in *Brewster* and one of *McCabe*'s saloon keepers, roles that in their gentleness and essential normality ill-prepared a viewer to confront the near-psychopathic intensity Schuck brought to his portrayal of Chicamaw. Remsen's previous roles for Altman are closer to the gleefully dumb loser he plays

Chicamaw (John Schuck) rehearses a bank robbery with the kids

in *Thieves*: the vicious, bigoted cop in *Brewster* and the zinc miner in *McCabe* who's pathetically grateful to see his mail-order bride (played by Shelley Duvall). And to his later parts: the dumb hick farmer in *Nashville* and the observer-bartender in *Buffalo Bill*. Remsen also played the timid transvestite in *California Split*, but this role has no associations with the other parts he's played for Altman. Michael Murphy explained how Remsen came to work in Altman's films: "Bert's story is especially nice, in that he was really through with the business. He wasn't acting any more; he was casting. He was coming back from lunch one day and a crane fell on him at Warner Brothers. He broke his back. It was terrible, and so Warner gave him a job casting when he got out of the hospital. He cast for years, and he was down in Houston casting *Brewster McCloud* and Bob said, 'Well, why don't you play it?' So he did *Brewster* and he went on, and now he's a fairly hot actor—and a *wonderful* actor. I'm thrilled for him."

Schuck, the decent, poker-loving nice guy of *M*A*S*H*, has been converted into a blubbery, drunken oaf in *Thieves*. Chicamaw has a perpetually turned-down mouth, as though he's sneering or dissatisfied, a Southern rube accent, and slicked-down hair as though he fancies himself a ladies' man. His behavior as he forces Mattie's children Bubba and Noel Joy to help him (and T-Dub) practice robbing banks is typical of his lack of restraint, his unsocialized primitiveness. When the kids don't want to play any more, Chicamaw becomes uncontrollaby angry; he's like a child himself, he can't stand being thwarted. Expediency is the hallmark of the sociopath, as Chicamaw demonstrates when, instead of stopping to talk to the cops after Bowie's accident, he shoots them and makes his getaway. Similarly, while he and the other two are robbing a bank, a bank officer reaches for the alarm, and rather than rip out the wire or club the man into submission, Chicamaw and Remsen find it simpler just to shoot him in the back. Chicamaw likes his life as a criminal; he remembers with relish the time he had a machine gun in his hands—he didn't get to fire it, but it was a high point in his life nevertheless. If T-Dub is the brains and Bowie is the neophyte of the gang, then Chicamaw is the brawn, a function he describes when talking of himself: "There's only three things in the world that I love to do, that's love, drink, and rob banks." If Bowie is the tyro in the group, then he's too dumb to pull off Chicamaw's rescue from the state penitentiary, a coup he does in fact effect, to Chicamaw's enormous chagrin. Calling Bowie a "country chump," he declares, "I don't see how you do it," and angrily denounces Bowie for making him look like thirty cents. With T-Dub dead at this point, Bowie's ties to his gang are virtually severed, and having engineered his old buddy's escape, he hauls the trigger-happy Chicamaw, who has just murdered the warden they took along as a hostage, from the car and leaves him ranting on a back-country road.

Vincent Canby appraised the performances for the *New York Times*: "All of the performances are quite special. Bert Remsen is fine as T-Dub. John Schuck, as Chicamaw, is extraordinary in the film's key scene near the end. Society doesn't destroy these men. The Depression may have given them a push into their chosen professions, but they are, at heart, so self-destructive that I'm not at all sure they wouldn't have wound up much the same had they been farmers." Pauline Kael, writing in the *New Yorker*, also lauded the acting: "John Schuck has also turned up in other Altman films, but there was nothing in his earlier work to prepare one for his major performance here, in the pivotal role of the heavy-drinking, half-mad Chicamaw. Schuck has always had a suggestion of a bulldog in his face, and now, grown corpulent and more powerful-looking, he gives a performance that in some scenes rivals the intensity that Bogart brought to his Fred C. Dobbs in *The Treasure of the Sierra Madre*. Schuck's comic, terrifying big scene, when he insists on play-acting a robbery at home with small children and explodes in a murderous rage when they lose interest, and his last scene, in which he's deserted, yelling in torment on a country road, are classic moments."

T-Dub is supposed to be the brains of the outfit, the older man with all the experience, but he's a bumbling fool, a man so dumb that when he marries Lula he puts his real name on the license. Lula is what passes for a femme fatale in Altman's world of failures, misfits, and buffoons. With her put-on air of stylishness, conferred by being a student at a beauty academy, her kimonos and her streaked, half-dyed hair, Lula drives T-Dub mad with desire, and soon he's spending more time mauling her than planning robberies. His brightest moment comes when he declares, in a flash of surprising intuition, "I should have robbed people with my brain instead of a gun." He is killed at the end by methods unspecified, presumably the victim of the same self-destructive urges that let him get hitched up with Lula and to become involved with a half-mad robber and a kid. But while he lives, he plans the jobs that land the "gang" on the front pages of Southern newspapers, gleefully chortling, like a litany, "This'll be my 30th [31st, 32nd, etc.] bank!"

The Depression-inspired thirst for heroes and exciting headlines is an important facet of *Thieves Like Us*. The men's pictures appear in the papers and detective

Ann Latham and Bert Remsen

magazines, and their exploits are broadcast on the radio, as much because there's a dearth of salable news as because they're important criminals. Theirs is a manufactured notoriety, but, like the fate that accrues to Bonnie and Clyde, it is not the cause of their downfall. Mattie turns Bowie in because she's afraid his crimes and her association with a criminal will affect her impressionable children and her husband, who is himself in prison.

Mattie is another force to be reckoned with. She keeps her family together while her man is away and provides a home for the men while they're waiting to pull their next theft. Louise Fletcher was producer Jerry Bick's wife, and she went on location with the film in Mississippi. She had been an actress, so Altman asked her to play Mattie, which was originally a small role. When he saw how effective she was, he enlarged the part, which evolved into one of the focal points of the film. As Pauline Kael wrote, "Louise Fletcher has a full, strong body and great rounded arms; her Mattie is a no-nonsense woman who looks as if she had lived through what women in soap operas prattle about. She's a tough-broad earth mother with a coating of banal self-respectability—an authentic American-woman character." (She was supposed to play the role in *Nashville* that Lily Tomlin did, the mother of the deaf children. It was written for her, as she is herself the daughter of deaf parents. Her parents' disability provided an especially moving moment during the 1976 Academy Awards when she won the Oscar for best actress for *One Flew Over the Cuckoo's Nest* and thanked them for their support in sign language.)

Fletcher is one of the rocks upon which Altman has anchored his *Thieves Like Us*. Mattie is a woman who is struggling to keep her family together, to keep her head up in a community that must know her husband is in jail, and to give her children what she thinks are high-toned airs and graces. Pudgy Noel Joy practices tap dancing and the piano, and Bubba is exhorted to stop playing with firecrackers—explosives to Mattie presumably having associations with guns and death. Mattie provides refuge and hot meals during the long boring months while the men are hiding out, but after T-Dub's death she can't take it any more, her longing for peace and security overcomes her loyalty to the gang—or what's left of it—and she turns Bowie in. Louise Fletcher makes Mattie a woman of understandable, if not always admirable, strength and dignity.

Keechie and Bowie (Shelley Duvall and Keith Carradine)

Louise Fletcher restrains Shelley Duvall from going to the aid of Keith Carradine

The three robbers and the people they live with inhabit a self-enclosed environment, inadvertently locked into a cycle of killing and theft without outside references. All they know are banks, guns, and stifling houses; they're too ignorant to escape the crooked life and too used to quick riches to want to. But Altman has not made this an atmosphere of hellish claustrophobia. There are always cars, those grand thirties roadsters which sweep them from robbery to robbery and, clumsily, into destruction, and the lush Mississippi countryside, green, moist, and summery, an Eden which they seldom enjoy, staying cooped up in service stations, houses, and motels. Only Bowie, who plays ball on the grass outside his sylvan retreat, takes advantage of nature, the rest preferring booze and lustful grapplings inside the succession of stifling houses they inhabit. But even the fields offer no respite, for these are people who are literally doomed, by themselves, by other people, and by their own lack of sophistication. They seem to have no choice but to career headlong into their own annihilation, and to epitomize this condition there is no better symbol than Chicamaw, raving in fury, "Bowie! Bowie! Bowie!" as he stands spraddled in the middle of the dirt road, abandoned, watching the back of Bowie's car as Bowie rides off in disgust at Chicamaw's lack of appreciation for being sprung from prison.

For these shimmering views of rural Mississippi, Altman has the team of French cinematographer Jean Boffety and production designer Jack de Govia to thank. When Mark Rydell, who had acted for Altman in his previous film, *The Long Goodbye*, hired Altman's regulars, Vilmos Zsigmond and Leon Ericksen, to work on *Cinderella Liberty*, Altman was left without the keystones of his regular crew. But Boffety and de Govia were felicitous choices to take the places of the men who had served Altman well in the past. They created a glowing, but not too pretty, locale for Edward Anderson's small, personal tragedy, a tragedy that was echoed in the poor reception the public gave Altman's near-perfect drama of crime and deceit in rustic America. The reviews were magnificent, but the paying customers stayed away in droves.

Jon Landau of *Rolling Stone* said, "Altman has become best known for his unique sense of period, striking use of color, rambling way with a story, and unusual emphasis on detail. Some have made the mistake of concluding that his style is an end in itself, but the real beauty of his best films—and *Thieves Like Us* is the best I've seen—rests in his integration of all elements until they become inseparable... And the film is no less interesting for what Altman chooses to omit. For example, *Thieves Like Us* contains not one adult who could serve as a reasonably healthy model for the two." Vincent Canby found that "*Thieves Like Us* is not so perverse and witty as *The Long Goodbye*, nor is it so ambitious as *McCabe and Mrs. Miller*, but it is a more perfectly integrated work. It is full of things to think about that hang in the memory like the details of a banal crime story on page 32, which though read quickly, won't go away. Somehow you know that this happened. It makes me suspect that, without telling us, the director has embarked on a project to define in his films what loftily might be defined as the American Experience."

Pauline Kael declared that "It's a serenely simple film—contained and complete. You feel elated by the chasteness of the technique, and the film engages your senses and stays with you, like a single vision. Robert Altman finds a sureness of tone and never loses it. . . . *Thieves Like Us* seems to achieve beauty without artifice. It's the closest to flawless of Altman's films—a masterpiece."

Altman himself provides an explanation for his characters' behavior: "What I saw in the film was: You really liked these people and you really felt sorry for them and their dilemma. I thought it was a real look at the society thirty years from [*McCabe and Mrs. Miller*], the way it developed with free enterprise. I thought *Thieves Like Us* was a great document on America at that time. It was just the beginning of communications, radio was just coming into its own. Advertising was coming in. People were starting to behave the way they were told to behave, and yet there was no way out from poverty for those people, who were poor and uneducated.

"I think that Bowie became twisted, and Keechie, I didn't see her as particularly sympathetic. I saw her as selfish, wanting what she wanted, wanting what she saw as her world. She is a survivor. With Bowie and Keechie, when they are together there is safety, and although it wasn't happiness, at least it was the absence of unhappiness."

California Split

Although Altman calls *California Split* "a celebration of gambling," the film is virtually the opposite: a cheerless look at gambling's obsessive players and their compulsion to lie to themselves that everything will be all right if they can change their luck, raise enough cash to get into a high-stakes game, keep their own spirits high so superstition won't weigh them down, or simply not think about any of these things so they can concentrate on the game at hand.

Altman follows two outwardly different (and inwardly similar) players to show what a dedicated gambler's life is like, what it comprises: fear, hope, anxiety, jubilation, and deception; and what it excludes: love, peace, closeness, trust, and relaxation.

Charlie Waters (Elliott Gould) meets Bill Denny (George Segal) playing poker at a club, where Charlie goads a sore loser, Lew (Edward Walsh), into a fight. Charlie and Bill become friendly at a nearby bar; the sore loser has them robbed and beaten in a parking lot, and Charlie takes Bill to his house to recuperate. Charlie shares the home of two soft-core hookers, Barbara Miller (Ann Prentiss) and Susan Peters (Gwen Welles), who took *him* home one night when he paid their rent.

Bill is already in trouble with his job—he's an editor for a magazine whose proprietor would like to see him at his

Charlie (Elliott Gould) and Bill (George Segal) in CALI-FORNIA SPLIT

desk more often—and with his bookie, Sparkie (played by the scriptwriter, Joseph Walsh, whose real-life brother plays Lew), whom he has owed $2,200 for a long time. He's separated from his wife; no conclusions are drawn from this, but one is allowed to infer that she left him because of his addiction.

Charlie is a so-called free spirit, content to live off his two roommates, with whom he is avuncular rather than romantic. Charlie supplies Barbara and Susan with advice and comfort. They keep him in beer, Froot Loops, and a place to lay his curly black hair.

California Split is plotless and eventful, as are most Altman films, and the events range from singing and drinking in the parking lot where they're robbed through an exchange with a terrified transvestite, Helen (Bert

Gwen Welles and Elliott Gould

Remsen), who has come to take the girls to Chasen's, to Charlie's revenge on Lew at the track, where he beats him up, takes his money, and leaves him on the men's-room floor, advising him to stuff toilet paper up his nose to stop the bleeding. The chronicle ends in Las Vegas with Bill's triumph at poker, craps, roulette, and blackjack, a winning streak that nets the two pals a total of $82,000 and a letdown that not even Charlie's habitually hyper personality can rise above.

Altman accumulates the details of Charlie and Bill's joint adventures (like most Altman characters they are finite—what brought then to this stage and what will transpire afterward are of little or no importance) until a portrait of their divergent and similar obsessions emerges. The differences between the men are those of style, not degree. Seemingly more rabid than Charlie, Bill is only more open in expressing his fears and reluctance to take a chance. Charlie will bet on anything anywhere; Bill likes to think things over, weigh the odds, worry, and then bet anyway. Both are basically childlike in that they refuse to see the real world as anything more than a backdrop for their passion; everything refers to them and their needs. They are like selfish, asocial youngsters squabbling over the rules of a game as life in its richness and variety passes them by unnoticed.

Charlie talks to himself, to strangers, to inanimate objects, in a way that is not so much whistling in the dark as it is a need to establish contact, no matter how fleeting, with the world around him. This is an outgrowth of Gould's personality that Altman used in *The Long Goodbye* and *M*A*S*H*, where both Gould and Donald Sutherland kept up running monologues with the air.

Charlie is a born kibitzer, an "arranger," as evidenced by the scene on the bus going to the track, where he devises a complicated scheme for exchanging seats to make various riders happy, simultaneously touting a young lady off Egyptian Femme—then betting on the horse himself and winning, to her vigorously expressed anger. He also arranges, with Bill, to spoil the girls' date with Helen, for purely selfish reasons—they've just won at the track and want to celebrate with Barbara and Susan— by posing as members of the vice squad and scaring the timid transvestite off.

Part of Charlie's kibitzing is to bet on anything that's going. When he and Bill take the girls to the fights, he bets on a bout with the man in front of him—for the man's cap. An altercation in the stands between two spectators calls for an immediate side bet. While waiting for Bill to hock his possessions to raise the money for the Las Vegas game,

Gould and Segal at the track

Charlie bets on the number of baskets he can make with some young turks who think Charlie is an "old man." But the bets are almost meaningless, off-the-cuff actions, made to keep his agile mind in motion and his glib tongue talking. Charlie is as hooked on gambling as Bill is, but ebulliently, without Bill's depressed sense of futility.

Charlie and Bill together are a single manic-depressive individual. Charlie alone is manic, his external high spirits covering the emptiness of his life. But Charlie's life does not have to be "full" of the things so-called normal people value. His head is full of temporary fantasies involving betting or raising money to gamble with.

Charlie's desperation is a means of getting high, of elevating himself psychically by sheer force of his imagination. He is able to project himself into the fantasies of those around him—whether it's Bill, whom he

can goad into taking chances, or Susan, whom he cheers up by telling a fable because he understands how she's been hurt and how her mind will respond to his efforts. It's Charlie's free-wheeling imagination that inspires Bill and propels him to win in Vegas. Without Charlie, Bill can't make it. He lacks faith in himself, the imagination to see himself as a winner. For Charlie, all things are possible, and it is his confidence that Bill rides to victory in an incredible winning streak. "I've got the heat!" he chortles to Charlie, but refuses to let Charlie have any money to play with or to watch him play while he's amassing his first $11,000. Charlie distracts him and is banished to the slot machines. He turns up while Bill is playing roulette and brings bad luck. "You're going to kill the streak!" yells Bill, sunk in superstition and the conviction that everything he touches will turn to gold. Bill has learned how to roll with his luck; Charlie wants to take the $11,000 and have a good time; Bill sees that he can take this farther and run it into a comparative fortune. Charlie enables Bill to make the quantum leap from small-time loser (and occasional winner) to big-time winner—who still has the natural outlook of a loser, for when all is said and done, Bill is no happier as a success than he was unhappy as a failure. He just has more money. But it was never the money that was the real goal, although neither man knew it. It was "the heat," the idea of winning, the vision of himself as what he always wanted to be—a big winner. Winning is an empty victory, since it takes the edge off his high. As Charlie notes, "Do you always take a big win this hard?" and Bill rejoins, "There was no special feeling. I just said there was," as he tries to comprehend the nature of his letdown, his betrayal by his own steamed-up energies. For Bill has used up his future. Once he's won, there's nothing left to hope and connive for. Winning is ultimately as demoralizing as defeat was. All he can do is quit in defeated exhaustion and go home. "Where do you live?" Charlie asks sarcastically. Bill is quitting too soon for Charlie, who has more hope and vitality to invest in Bill's freaky success, as well as a half share in the profits.

Bill Denny and Charlie Waters are opposite sides of the same coin. Tense, nervous, debt-haunted Bill can't believe the relaxed, jiving Charlie is for real. "Where do you get your confidence?" he asks at one point, his face betraying his half-admiring incredulity. George Segal plays Bill with mannerisms that are familiar from other characterizations, but seem to belong particularly to this anxious, crumple-browed loner. In their first encounter, while Charlie is assaulting Lew across the poker table, Bill the coward collects his chips from the table and crawls away across the floor. His hunched shoulders and permanently worried expression are a direct contrast to Charlie's gum-chewing, singing openness.

Charlie, who likes to live "close to the action" and doesn't have a car, drags Bill home with him and introduces him to the wonderful world of Froot Loops and beer for breakfast. Charlie understands Bill immediately, noting, "Nobody's going to tell your mother," when Bill checks to see if the hot lather Charlie has applied to his sore abdomen (after their fracas with Lew and his hired thugs in the parking lot) is staining his sweater.

Their friendship is cemented through their shared mania, their complimentary personalities, and their aversion to the straight world. Bill is a liar when necessary, as when he declares that it was car trouble that kept him from the office, or when he invents an excuse to get away from his job and go to the track with Charlie. In spite of the proximity of Barbara and Susan, Bill is no more interested in sex than Charlie is, although he makes a halfhearted pass at Susan. Like Charlie, Bill is beyond sex; his libido has been superseded by his warped ego.

Although Bill lives in a state of permanent suspicion and doubt, he trusts Charlie. It is his faith in Charlie's belief in him that enables him to win in Las Vegas. Without Charlie, Bill would still be a psychically crippled loser; with Charlie, he can make the imaginative leap to confidence and victory. With Charlie he can relax temporarily, pound the piano, and sing "Rustus Rastus Johnson Brown," or roust Helen with their shared pretense of being vice-squad cops.

Charlie is easily distracted; Bill is all tense concentration and single-mindedness. When he hocks his car to raise the money for Vegas, it's exactly the sum he owes his bookie. But it never occurs to him to pay Sparkie back, in spite of his promises. And although the audience isn't led to speculate on the protagonists' lives beyond the confines of what's on the screen, it's impossible not to believe that Bill and Charlie will gamble away their winnings, retaining their poker-palace pallor rather than enjoying the California sunlight they never seem to spend much time in.

The girls Charlie lives with are female mirror-images of Charlie and Bill. They are both unprofessional call girls, but Barbara is a little more together than Susan. Barbara is much like Charlie; her casual demeanor reflects his as she smokes while slopping milk into Bill's cereal. She mothers and reassures Susan much as Charlie "fathers" and inspirits Bill. As Susan says, "She takes care of everything." Barbara and Charlie have even spent time in jail in New York; they reminisce about the food there.

Charlie and Bill manage to intimidate the girls' "date,"
Helen Brown (Bert Remsen)

Segal and Gould

A scene deleted from the finished print of CALIFORNIA SPLIT

Like Charlie, Barbara has an instinct for survival. She refuses to cancel the date with Helen because Helen has promised the girls "$150 apiece for dinner."

Susan resembles Bill. Her childish insistence on being liked for herself is similar to Bill's belief that he can get away with murder at work and with his bookie. Susan is the "baby of the house," an idea reinforced by her appearing in Dr. Dentons complete with feet and climbing on a chair to get "her" cereal bowl while Bill watches in disbelief from the couch. Like Bill, Susan hopes for a better future, but doesn't really have much faith in the idea, and like Bill—before he meets Charlie— she takes no initiative. Like a child, she cheers at the fights with her eyes closed, happy to be with the grownups but unwilling to watch the bloodshed.

Altman has said of his film, "*California Split* doesn't make a moral judgment, it simply mirrors the atmosphere and kind of world that gamblers function in." The atmosphere Altman refers to is a largely indoors, nighttime arena of poker palaces, prizefights, and bars, with an occasional look at the outdoors as the men go to the track, play basketball, or get robbed in a parking lot. But it is always the seedy, desperate atmosphere surrounding the confirmed gambler which is at the center of this world. Altman never strays from his subject—even Helen is gambling. She gets up the nerve to be seen in public dressed as a woman, only to have her plans foiled by Bill and Charlie and her own cowardice.

As in many Altman films (*Nashville* and *Buffalo Bill and the Indians*, for example) a "show" motif is part of the film's backdrop. In this case, it introduces the audience to the film and to the world of gambling. At the poker club, where the film starts, a slide show explains how poker is played and the niceties of poker behavior. As the show's voice-over continues, Altman's camera enters the club and picks up various players, many of whom are violating those canons of desirable conduct. The most noticeable exponent of card-playing misconduct is Lew, the sore loser, whose violent temper disrupts the game.

Altman also uses the songs of Phyllis Shotwell, who has an appropriately coarse and ironic voice, as a commentary on the action. When the men are robbed a second time in a parking lot, she is heard singing from "Ace in the Hole," "This town is full of guys who think they're mighty wise..." The song is carried over to the next scene, in the poker parlor, and she now comments, "If he lost that old ace down in the hole..." as the camera shows Bill, whose eyes shift worriedly as he has a losing streak at cards. Shotwell is seen playing at her Vegas piano bar; she's a philosophical type who has seen everything and makes no judgments on the behavior of

Elliott Gould: on a winning streak at last

the gamblers around her.

Altman's own proclivity for gambling is well known. As he says, "It's something I really like. I like to play poker, I like going to the races, but I can't allocate any time to it. I love betting on football! Year before last, I won about twenty-six thousand dollars—but I never stop while I'm winning. I may bet five hundred or a thousand dollars on a game, but you always lose in the long run because of the percentages." But Altman's real gambles these days are with his movies. He takes chances that the public will try to understand what he's doing, will see that his free-form exercises, like *California Split*, are intended

George Segal

as entertainment and are not merely obscure, rambling improvisations meant for a coterie of initiates who will accept anything the master produces.

The critics liked *California Split* and it made the *New York Times* ten-best-film list; according to *Variety* it has earned upwards of five million dollars. Vincent Canby of the *Times* said, "Mr. Altman has been quoted as saying that *California Split* is 'a celebration of gambling,' which is, I think, to underrate it, at least to someone who is not a gambling nut. The director, his screenwriter, Joseph Walsh, and the actors have created a movie of so many associations that it's impossible not to see *California Split* as something much more complex and disturbing.

"*California Split* is sometimes very funny, but the world it depicts is as bleak as a landscape composed entirely of used-car lots. The present tense for everyone in the film is grim. The clocks are out of sync. Someone says of a poker game, 'It just got started yesterday.' The compulsive gambler will put up with any loss or indignity in the hope of recouping later, thus placing a terrible burden on the future. For once he does win, everything is over."

Nashville

When the *New York Times* assigns Tom Wicker to write a Sunday "think piece" about a film, rather than using its regular critic, readers are being signaled that the film is "significant." Wicker, who is noted for his reporting on the Attica prison uprising of 1971, called *Nashville* "a two-and-a-half hour cascade of minutely detailed vulgarity, greed, deceit, cruelty, barely contained hysteria, and the frantic lack of root and grace into which American life has been driven by its own heedless vitality."

Pauline Kael of the *New Yorker*, who alternates her critical chores with Penelope Gilliatt, was scheduled to be on vacation when the film came out, but she reviewed it anyway, in a piece called "Coming: *Nashville*." Her preview (based on a six-hour rough cut) caused as much controversy as the film did, with *The Times*'s Vincent Canby suggesting sarcastically that reviews could be written on the basis of a comma or a concept. Four months later, when Gilliatt's review appeared, she called *Nashville* a film "about the cement filling in a decayed tooth, about effort annulled by void, about the nothing that comes of nothing." None of the reviewers said that *Nashville* was funny, but they heaped every other adjective they could locate upon it, with the result that

Henry Gibson and Barbara Baxley (right) welcome Ronee Blakely back to Nashville

Young hopeful and old hopeful: Gwen Welles and Keenan Wynn in NASHVILLE

Altman's film, while obviously a sturdy specimen, was made to bear too heavy a critical load, and some audiences felt they hadn't experienced the exhilaration they'd been led to expect they would.

In *Nashville* Altman has expanded his field of vision to encompass twenty-four characters as they pass the days directly preceding a political rally for Hal Phillip Walker, the Replacement Party's candidate for President. John Triplette (Michael Murphy), Walker's advance man, scours the country-and-western bars, the pickin' parlors, and the homes of Nashvillians, trying to round up an impressive display of talent for Walker's appearance at the Nashville Parthenon. The film begins with the dawn departure of Walker's sound truck from its garage and ends with Walker himself departing the Parthenon in his sleek black limousine following the assassination of Barbara Jean (Ronee Blakely), the leading lady of the Nashville sound. In between, Altman focuses on the performers encountered either by Triplette or by Opal, a nitwit interviewer for the BBC (Geraldine Chaplin).

Opal has come to Nashville to do a documentary, lugging her tape recorder and her preconceived notions like so much excess baggage. She's like a migratory drone, permanently weighed down by everything she owns, which she's carting around with her. She's a mass of pins and scarves and bracelets, her microphone thrust before her and her opinions unfurled like so many aggressive banners. Opal is impervious to the truth or to the evidence of her own eyes, as indicated by the way she exaggerates the extent of a highway pile-up for the sake of her report. "It's America," she coos, lying glibly about mangled bodies and smashed cars. But America is the deaf children of Linnea (Lily Tomlin), a gospel singer, or being used (as Opal is) by Tom (Keith Carradine) the stud rock star. But neither idea is one Opal is capable of facing.

Every so often a genuine perception creeps into Opal's stream-of-unconsciousness prattle, as when she observes to Triplette that ordinary citizens like Lady Pearl (Barbara Baxley) and "all these people here in this country who carry guns are the real assassins because they stimulate the other innocent people who eventually are the ones who pull the trigger." At this point Altman cuts to a shot of Kenny (David Hayward), the moony young man who boards with Keenan Wynn (playing Mr. Green). As Kenny talks to his mother on the phone, L.A. Joan (Shelley Duvall) picks up Kenny's violin case. Although Altman makes no visual comment on this scene, we know from its juxtaposition with the previous one (and from our own memories of similar sinister violin cases in the movies of the past) that it has significance.

Opal, of course, turns out to be correct, when one of the "ordinary citizens" reveals himself as a killer—one of the "innocent people" urged to action by the atmosphere around him. Opal misses the killing, having ducked into a television truck to change the film in her camera. While trying to communicate with one audience, she fails to perceive a more important message—Kenny's revelation of his ill-focused antipathy toward the woman who is confused in his mind with both his overbearing mother and the symbols around him of overwhelming political power.

Triplette gambles on his handling of the televised Walker rally to make his career in politics. Triplette is a politician—whatever will succeed is what he's promoting (like *Buffalo Bill*, who would proclaim a year later that "Truth is whatever gets the loudest applause"), whether it's the promise of a governorship for Haven Hamilton (Henry Gibson) to lure him to the Parthenon, or the

Henry Gibson and Michael Murphy

Dave Peel and Geraldine Chaplin

promise of being on the same stage as Barbara Jean so that Sueleen Gay (Gwen Welles) will strip at the political smoker and it will be a success in raising money for Walker.

John Triplette is a charming, cynical opportunist who uses everyone around him to get his way, first fawning on country-and-western stars so they'll appear for Walker, then calling their music "redneck" and "crapola" so that Mary and Bill, rock neophytes, will also perform at the rally.

He's a blandly calculating exponent of the least-resistance school of political advancement. Strippers, gospel singers, blacks, Triplette wants everyone on the stage, not for Walker, but for himself. He's a gambler, and this is his chance to make it big.

Murphy remembers talking over his role with Altman: "I remember there was a big discussion about me, when I went to the Grand Ole Opry, getting dressed up in a cowboy outfit. I said 'Jesus, the guy would just never give up that identity, that physical look that he had.' [Altman said] 'You're right. That's right!' There was an awful lot of [his role] that you don't see in the picture. There were moments where he told about his background a little bit. He was divorced and his wife ran off with an actor and all this shit. So you kind of knew where he was, and yet, even though this information isn't supplied, you still know something about that guy by just watching him walk around. It came out of scenes we improvised and played with and talked about and a lot of just thinking about these characters."

The other political opportunist is Haven Hamilton who, like Barbara Jean, dresses exclusively in white, perhaps as a symbol of his intentionally inoffensive blandness, perhaps to match the milk he tosses down while others are drinking hard liquor. Although Hamilton exudes wholesome all-American purity and sanctimonious virtues, he is, in fact, a self-satisfied egomaniac, ruthlessly overriding everyone's wishes as he manipulates those around him to get his own way. His remark about his son, Buddy (Dave Peel), "We're just trying to give him the breaks we never got," casually ignores the idea that Buddy may have his own ambitions, which have been subverted to his father's implacable prerogatives. Although Buddy seems sincere when he tells Opal that handling his father's business affairs is "great. It really is. You know, Dad's wanted me to do that all his life," his manner accidentally betrays his dissatisfaction with his life, a notion that is reinforced by Buddy telling Opal that his father would never allow him to be a singer. Buddy proceeds to sing "The Heart of a Gentle Woman" in a sincere, touching way that indicates that it comes from *his* heart, and is probably an example of the one thing he would genuinely like to do and which is denied him. Opal herself denies Buddy the opportunity to sing by interrupting him to corner Elliott Gould; she has only been using Buddy anyway, as a means of getting to his father.

Haven Hamilton's white clothes seem to be a conscious denial of others' negative images; *he*, at least, is the picture of propriety. His untarnished respectability is undermined somewhat by the presence of his mistress, Lady Pearl, although this side of his life is presumably kept from his fans.

The toupee that doesn't quite match his hair is another example of his inability to see himself clearly. He's a paragon of rectitude and fairness, to himself; to others, he's a short, faintly foolish individual dressed in clothes too young and gaudy for his years. He's an unctuous hypocrite who plays every situation for what it's worth—to him. But at the end he rises above his own self-aggrandizing image to achieve a stature and grace not indicated by his previous behavior. Ignoring his own wound, Hamilton takes charge and brings order out of the chaos both onstage and in the audience, telling the crowd, "This isn't Dallas, this is Nashville. . . . You show 'em what we're made of," and telling Albuquerque (Barbara Harris), "You stay here and sing." Hamilton is no longer a self-important caricature but a figure of dignity and integrity, helping to bind others' emotional wounds even as his own blood flows.

Lady Pearl, habitually dressed in purple, is Hamilton's consort, his son's surrogate mother, and his own semiofficial manageress. Although she presides over her own club, Lady Pearl devotes herself to functioning as Hamilton's mistress, bouncer, and social watchdog. When Hamilton, thinking only in terms of racial stereotypes, offers some watermelon to the black singer, Tommy Brown (Timothy Brown), Lady Pearl smacks his hand and remedies the situation by giving Brown lettuce instead. She has a long monologue about the dead Kennedy brothers that is as foolish as it is moving. It's clear that she's crying to show the embarrassed Opal, who didn't know what she was getting into, that she *cares* about politics, that the men's deaths were a horrible loss. It's a demonstration, but Barbara Baxley's rueful exasperation makes it something more than just emotional showing off.

Albuquerque, whose real, down-home name, Wini-fred, is closer to the plain truth of her life as a redneck farmer's wife than to her vision of herself as a country-and-western star, looks like a tattered kewpie doll, a Daisy Mae with a hysterical mop of blond straw for hair.

Keith Carradine: "I'm Easy"

Even more than the no-talent Sueleen, Albuquerque wants to be a star and rises stunningly to the occasion, rallying the crowd at the Parthenon with her stirring, healing anthem, "It Don't Worry Me." It doesn't matter that she isn't a good singer; when she has to pitch in, she looses her fuzzy-brained softness and becomes a manipulative siren of a singer, forcing the crowd to forget the tragedy they've just seen and become a unit, a power that can overcome the senseless murder. She reaches into the audience, pulling out responses from some wellspring of her own need to perform.

Albuquerque's lack of focus is related to Sueleen's. Sueleen will do anything to become a star except face the fact that she has no talent and give up while she still has a vestige of pride. Albuquerque has no pride, and no real sense of direction, as evidenced by her remark to Kenny, when they meet by the highway, "I'm on my way to town to become a country-music singer or a star." Anything will do as long as it's an escape from her crude, unsympathetic husband, Star (Bert Remsen).

Sueleen Gay is a shameless fool; she's got a hide so thick she doesn't know her songs are drivel, that the mincing, posturing act she's pieced together out of other performers' mannerisms was old stuff five years ago, and that nobody wants to see a singer whose bra is stuffed with gym socks. She's eternally optimistic; her fantasy life enables her to not believe in the truth about herself even when Wade (Robert Doqui), who loves her and wants to help her, tells her flat-out that she has no talent. But her bungled striptease almost lets her see herself for what she is; unfortunately, she achieves her objective—being on the same platform as Barbara Jean—so she can laugh at Wade's "truth" and ignore her own.

Barbara Jean is as beautiful and as fragile emotionally as she appears to be physically. She wears long, virgin-white dresses and bows in her hair like a country-and-western Mary Pickford. She has a welcoming smile for everyone and takes a sincere interest in other people, as evidenced by her asking Mr. Green if his wife is taking her Vitamin E in the hospital where both are patients.

Barbara Jean's tenuous grip on reality is revealed at the Opry Belle where, in her reminiscences about her childhood, she hints at the route which led to her present precarious psychic state. Her rambling monologue about working since she was a youngster concludes with her asking her husband (Allen Garfield as Barnett) "Am I all right?"—an indication of how far out of touch with herself she is. Her lack of awareness about her own condition makes it all the more easy for Barnett to exploit her. He has managed her career, and somehow this crass, greasy man has also managed to marry her. Barnett knows how insecure Barbara Jean's grasp on the real world is because he helped to bring her to this predicament through his ruthless but placating guidance of her talent and his manipulation of her frail psychological being. Her puppetlike responses to Barnett's questions about why he's going to thank Connie White (Karen Black) for appearing in her place are another example of her wind-up personality—for Barnett, Barbara Jean is a malleable child, but like a child, she's also willful and argumentative, a lovely toy child whose mechanism is running down.

Ronee Blakely's stunning scene on the Opry Belle shows her mind beginning to unravel as she slides into the safety of remembering her childhood, a time before she was on her own, pushed and prodded by people who do not have her best interests at heart. She makes a noise like a chicken, tells the audience about her grandmother's false teeth, and generally indicates that she's slipping fast. Altman recalls how he almost missed getting this scene on film: "Ronee Blakely caught me on the worst day, emotionally, of *Nashville*. In the script she's supposed to faint and they carry her off. I said, 'You fainted before. Why don't you just go catatonic?' The next morning we had a lot of problems and I was really, really down. It was stringing out toward the end of the picture. I was screaming on the telephone at somebody, and somebody else came in and said, 'Ronee wants to see you.' So I walked over to her and I said, 'Do you want to see me?' kind of gruffly. 'I suppose you've got ideas for the scene, huh?' So she took out this notebook and she started reading from this thing. I said, 'I don't know, Ronee, I've got too much. Let's just do what we're supposed to do.' She said, 'Okay, whatever you say.' I got to feeling bad about it and finally I said, 'Go ahead. Do what you were going to do.' Well, it's just dynamite material. And I sat there and I thought, 'I damn near blew this. I just damn near sat there and did not listen to this.' I came that close. It's some of the best stuff—it's remarkable."

Keith Carradine plays Tom, the third member of the rock group, Tom, Bill, and Mary, whose first record is displayed at the airport newsstand. He's a thoroughly repellent character, a priapic narcissist who screws women and throws them away like used Kleenex. One woman who survives his calculated onslaught is Linnea, the gospel-singing mother of two deaf children, who makes herself more attractive to Tom by refusing to date him. When she finally agrees to meet him, it's at one of downtown Nashville's country-and-western parlors. There he sings "I'm Easy" to her, while each of three other women in the room who have recently shared his bed choose to believe that his song is for her. At the motel, Linnea proves more resilient than the rest; she teaches him sign language and doesn't allow Tom to blackmail her emotionally into staying longer than she wants to. She's unruffled when he tries to get even with her for leaving by calling another girl (Tom rushes in fresh replacements whenever there's a lull).

Carradine describes Tom by saying, "The character was distasteful. I had a very difficult time with the role. I never did feel comfortable. I couldn't find anything in him that I could like, so that worked for itself. You saw an actor who didn't like what he was doing, so what it comes off as is a character who doesn't like himself."

Canby referred to Lily Tomlin's "spectacular dramatic debut," and Judith Crist, writing in *New York* magazine, said that Linnea's "dazzling beauty comes from her steadfast acceptance of defects in those she loves." Both Tomlin and Ronee Blakley were nominated as best actress by the Academy of Motion Picture Arts and Sciences, but they lost to Louise Fletcher of *One Flew Over the Cuckoo's Nest*, whom Altman had, ironically, coaxed from retirement for a small part in *Thieves Like Us*.

Ned Beatty plays Linnea's husband, like Allen Garfield's Barnett a plump, sweaty hustler, a man whose career has overridden all other considerations to the point that he's never taken the time to learn his children's sign language. Here, Altman makes an indirect comment on the ruthless priority success has—people are willing to dehumanize themselves and those around them for its sake. But Beatty's Delbert Reese isn't just a one-dimensional political striver. When he takes Sueleen home, he tries to comfort her, and in the desperation that fat men sometimes have for affection, tells her, "I'd like to kiss you everyplace—you know what I'm telling you?" But he's still a gentleman. Delbert is both reticent and urgent, gentle and hopeless, a romantic in the company of a fantasist. His scene at home with Linnea, in which she makes him wait to talk to her until after the children have told her about their swimming test, shows that he usually gets her attention second, and that for all the surface pleasantries, there probably isn't much warmth in this marriage.

Karen Black plays Connie White, the eternal second-runner to Barbara Jean's first lady. Connie wears a dress that looks like a Schrafft's Valentine's Day chocolate box, and the black roots of her honey-colored hair show. She's as tough as nails, and implacably rude to Barnett when he brings her a present for standing in for his ailing wife. She doesn't miss the chance to slur Julie Christie's looks when the actress drops into the King of the Road, and she reacts to Albuquerque's attempt to get close to the object of her

Barbara Harris: "It Don't Worry Me"

worship by smiling glassily and ignoring her. She gives the feeling that if she had the chance, she'd murder Barbara Jean and take over the number-one spot without a murmur from her conscience.

The peripheral characters swirling in the waves made by the country-and-western heavies are: Shelley Duvall as L.A. Joan, the dumb, boppy, C&W groupie with eyes like saucers and a body that suggests intentional starvation; the Tricycle Man (Jeff Goldblum), the ubiquitous magician who looks vaguely amphibian and never says a word; David Arkin, as Norman the driver, who is good-naturedly the butt of some very cruel humor and unwarranted put-downs; Cristina Raines, the Mary of Tom, Bill, and Mary, who loves Tom, but can't say it to his face, and who is mortified when Opal, in a post-coital confession, chirpily avers that she's been making it with Tom, too; Frog (Richard Baskin, the composer of most of the music that wasn't written by the performers themselves), the object of Hamilton's wrath in the opening recording-studio scene; and Pfc. Glenn Kelly (Scott Glenn), the military angel who hovers around Barbara Jean—his mother rescued her from the fire which she's recuperating from when she returns to Nashville.

Ostensibly, the twenty-four characters Altman assembled for the film are there because they are (a) C&W stars and satellites; and (b) intended to participate in the Parthenon rally for Hal Phillip Walker. The Walker platform, smugly describing itself as "New Roots for the Nation," is a populist pastiche made up of pieces from the campaigns of George McGovern, Eugene McCarthy, and George Wallace. Boiled down, the platform is mostly nonsense and hits a vein of truth about as often as Opal does. Utlimately it stands for very little, except for a simplistic and vague call to action on behalf of replacing the present administration's bureaucracy with Walker's brand of government, magically free of red tape. One doesn't even know what, beside the present regime, is being replaced by this third party. But the fervent music, with its slick blend of banal patriotism ("We must be doing something right to last two hundred years") is a metaphor for, and a counterpart of, the same jingoistic lack of thought that Altman believes underlies American political and social life. One can be assured, listening to Hamilton's song, that Walker approves of his message and his oleaginous sentimentality. Similarly, "Keep A-Goin'," which celebrates unblinking enterprise, "It Don't Worry Me," with its litany of mindless optimism, and "For the Sake of the Children," with its pervasive aura of self-sacrifice and moral rectitude, are emblematic of Walker's stance.

Altman's point throughout the film is that show-business types are indistinguishable from our politicians (sometimes they *are* our politicians)—they promise the same glamor, the same atmosphere of ease and grace, and are equally worthy targets for our bullets. Assassinating a pop singer promises the same cheap notoriety as killing a Kennedy, and erases the same kind of pain, the pain of seeing those who have more, who are more, and who will always be more than we can ever hope to be. Killing murders the future.

Kenny's fragmented point of view confuses Barbara Jean with the warm, giving mother who might be his overbearing, bossy mother. This bad mother is similarly associated with the unresponsive, unapproachable power of American politicians.

As Altman says, "It just seems like the proper place for me to be able to equate the analogy of our elected officials and politicians—which in many ways, I think, is a popularity contest—with the success of country-and-western music. As I say, eventually it's just a way of melding a whole view, my view, of that political climate in America today.

"Today, Nashville is a city of instant success. It's the Hollywood of forty years ago. Recording studios, singers, musicians are everywhere. You get off the bus carrying a guitar and, with luck, in two years you have a guitar-shaped swimming pool. I wanted to do *Nashville* to study our myths and our heroes and our hypocrisy. Because by the time we usually get around to studying our present, it's past, and the truth is buried so deep we can't even find it."

Altman also discussed his methodology in making the film: "We had so many stories we could cut to. Any time I would start to get restless with one character, I would cut over to another one. You set a boundary of sorts, and then tell the actors that as long as they stay within the boundaries, it's okay. It's when they start getting out and carrying the ball somewhere that you have to stop it. What we do is set up the arena and create an event. Then we cover it as if it were actually happening. But, of course, we just happen to have a little more control than in real life. I can say, 'Let's do it once again.'"

Critics were divided in their opinions of *Nashville*. Was it *the* movie of the seventies, the film all others would be measured against? Or was it an unfocused mess? Joel E. Siegel, writing in *Film Heritage*, called it "Gnashville" and said that it "fails because its view of people, individually and collectively, is so shallow, so lacking in detail and sympathy. It's like a series of bumper stickers—bright, flashy, paper-thin expressions of attitudes—soon past, soon forgotten."

Tom Wicker said that "this is a culture in which old

people are thrown aside as carelessly as Colonel Sanders chicken bones, patriotism and sentimentality salve the hideous wounds of progress, and madmen peer mildly from benign eyes just before they strike. The greatest reward in this world is prime time, the greatest achievement is visibility, the most profound corruption is not that of the conned, who march willingly into their delusions and falsities."

Penelope Gilliatt said "Technically and emotionally the film is a crowning work and a harbinger. This is one of the ways that films will go, and Altman will have been the first to be there. He uses every tool at his disposal, including, especially, his own experience...and he develops the possibilities of improvisation with un-matched invention and point, covering the takes with multitrack recording systems and with a large number of cameras going at once, so that no accident of post-Stanislavskian acting is lost." However, Gilliatt felt that "there is also a disastrously conceived parody of a chatty BBC interviewer in a hat, which ineptly takes on targets of hauteur and archness that have been more skillfully shot at for decades by more knowledgeable people."

Jay Cocks, writing in *Time*, said the film will be remembered as the "movie debut of Lily Tomlin, extraordinary in the role of an upper-middle-class suburban housewife who sings with a black gospel group [with] intelligence, a dead-on perception of people that can be funny or rueful (or both at once), a uniquely intriguing mixture of sensuality and chagrin. There is hardly a false moment in her performance, never a trace of calculation or caricature. She is a major actress."

Canby, in his regular review, remarked, "There are so many story lines in *Nashville* that one is more or less coerced into dealing in abstractions. *Nashville* is about

A look at the twenty-four characters of NASHVILLE

the quality of life of a segment of Middle American life. It's about ambition, sentimentality, politics, emotional confusion, empty goals, and very big business, in a society whose citizens are firmly convinced that the use of deodorants is next to godliness.

"*Nashville* doesn't make easy fun of these people. It doesn't patronize them. Along with their foolishness, it sees their gallantry.... The movie is amused by the maudlin sentiments and rhyme schemes [of "Two Hundred Years"]. But it also appreciates the song's stirring beat and the vast, earnest public for whom it will have meaning."

In his Sunday contemplation of *Nashville*, Canby called it "Altman's first unequivocal hit since he made *M*A*S*H* five years ago,... another extraordinary chapter in the director's continuing history of America seen largely through the stories of gallant losers.... There is no grand design in these films. . . . His concerns are most effectively expressed in stories about people who think they know exactly what they want. . . . There is the possibility of overinterpreting material that is so rich in associations. It would be a mistake to attribute to the film too many mystical metaphors about the American Experience. The most stunning aspects of *Nashville* are the performances and the music, which has a good deal to do with the excitement the film generates."

Altman has the last word on his film: "Most people are disturbed by my form, and then I keep pushing it forward more in each movie. *Nashville* is the culmination of it all, I think. But maybe there's enough music and razzle-dazzle this time."

The New York Film Critics appended a codicil, choosing *Nashville* the best picture, Altman the best director, and Lily Tomlin the best supporting actress.

And the Motion Picture Academy added a postscript nominating *Nashville* as the best picture. Altman as best director, both Lily Tomlin and Ronee Blakley as best supporting actress, and Keith Carradine's song, "I'm Easy," as best original song. Only "I'm Easy" won.

But the biggest aftershock of *Nashville* never came to pass. Altman made a deal with ABC to expand the film into a four-hour feature, which would be shown on two consecutive Sunday nights and include material deleted from his final cut. The editing was completed, but in Altman's words: "Meantime, a new executive has been hired to make those decisions, and that sounded a little racy to him, and now they've decided they're just going to cut the original version so that it fits their format and runs the way every other lousy movie does."

Buffalo Bill and the Indians, or, Sitting Bull's History Lesson

If *Nashville* was Altman's pre-Bicentennial slur on the American way of life, *Buffalo Bill* was a direct slap in the face at American history. If it was going to be a success, Altman couldn't have timed it better. The mood of national disenchantment was pervasive, and President Jimmy Carter's post-Watergate new broom seemed less likely to sweep clean than to simply sweep the dirt under the rug. But, for reasons that have never been clear, *Buffalo Bill* was, as Altman himself states it bluntly, a "failure." Whether *Buffalo Bill* was directly responsible for losing Altman the direction of E. L. Doctorow's *Ragtime* is a moot point. Equally problematical was Altman's conception of that film as a two-part opus which would require two separate admissions and two nights at the movies. This may be the only way Doctorow's panorama could be given the scope to do it justice, but it wasn't Dino De Laurentiis's idea of commercial filmmaking, and Altman was fired. The director received another blow when he found that he'd been outbid for the rights to Kurt Vonnegut, Jr.'s *Breakfast of Champions* even though Alan Rudolph had already completed a script.

In any event, *Buffalo Bill* is a fascinating film, as interesting in the ways it does not succeed as in the many more ways that it does. The critics found it droll and

Paul Newman and Joel Grey in BUFFALO BILL AND THE INDIANS

delightful. Vincent Canby, writing in the *New York Times*, said that "It may be the most original American film of the year," and *Newsweek*'s Jack Kroll stated, "This movie seethes with a civilized fullness of intelligence." Richard Schickel of *Time* magazine wrote that "America's most interesting active film maker, Robert Altman, has created a wry, sly, wise study of what fame does to people cursed with that most mixed of blessings. Buffalo Bill Cody (superbly played by Paul Newman) was a legend created out of flimsy cloth by a pulp writer and promoter named Ned Buntline (impersonated by Burt Lancaster) who lurks around the fringes of the film. Buntline serves as a kind of chorus, singing counterpoint to the sleazy commercial tones ... from Bill and his more sophisticated manipulators. They seem to really believe that Buffalo Bill's Wild West Show is indeed 'America's National Family.' They make it their business to paper over the fact that the star can no longer differentiate

Burt Lancaster as Ned Buntline

between the legend that has been created for him and the much plainer reality of his past."

Buffalo Bill's credits state that it was adapted from the play called *Indians*, by Arthur Kopit, in which Stacy Keach starred on Broadway. Altman claims that neither he nor Alan Rudolph, who wrote the screenplay with Altman, ever saw or read *Indians*, but it is nevertheless a remarkably faithful rendition of Kopit's play. *Indians* places more emphasis on the plight of the Indians and even has Buffalo Bill make an impassioned plea on their behalf. The speech is, in fact, much like the one Sitting Bull's interpreter tries to make to the President toward the end of the film.

William F. Cody is presented as being so caught up in creating his legend even as he lives it that he is unable to give credit where it is due, namely to the fertile imagination of Ned Buntline, whose imaginative exploitation of the dime novel was the medium for Bill's deification. As Buntline says, from his self-imposed exile in the bar, "Any man who figures he's gonna set the world on fire best not forget where he got the matches." Bill refuses to even talk to Buntline and foolishly allows him to stay at the bar, where he can chip away at Bill's legend from a safe distance.

Into the self-enclosed world, bounded on one side by the Mayflower, Bill's office-cum-living-quarters, and on the other by the arena where he and his troupe perform their gloriously fraudulent feats of daring, comes Sitting Bull (Frank Kaquitts) and his interpreter, William Halsey (Will Sampson). Their grip on reality is much firmer than his, which causes an immediate confrontation over who is bossing whom, and over which issues. Bull is a plain little man who makes Bill, with his embroidered buckskins, touched-up goatee, and flowing wig look like a pompous fool. But it doesn't matter, because it's Bill's show and he's determined to capitalize on the situation by placing the Indians in as bad a light as possible. Unfortunately Bull doesn't see himself in the same way, and the confrontation accelerates till each is humiliating the other as much as possible without actually being rude. The culmination of their foolishness comes during a photographic session with the entire company which reflects the class (or race) consciousness of the participants. Bill feels that Sitting Bull and Halsey shouldn't be seen so close to Annie Oakley (Geraldine Chaplin), who has taken up their cause against Bill. Halsey is adamant; Bull will move from his position for twenty-five American dollars. Bill mutters that he'll have the picture retouched, and poses with his pistol hand across his chest, conveying his notion of what an idol of the Gilded Age should look like. The whole enterprise is interrupted and destroyed by a telegram from President Grover Cleveland. When Halsey informs the photographer, "You may take the photograph," he and Sitting Bull are the only ones left. Altman's comment on the effect of celebrity is to demonstrate that the scramble for fame is meaningless because the next eminent person on the scene cancels out the one before, no matter how celebrated they might be.

Bull embarrasses Buffalo Bill, in front of one of the amorous sopranos Bill is forever wooing, by firing off one of Bill's pistols in the direction of a tent. The bullets make a widespread pattern on the canvas, proving that Bill's claim to unerring marksmanship is unwarranted—he's been using a scatter gun. Bull leaves to follow the moon to the mountains and Bill thinks he's absconded, so he and his minions take off in hot pursuit. (First, Bill storms around, shouting, "Where's my real jacket?" Then he frightens Lucille's pet bird, of which he has an irrational fear.) Later the entire camp turns out to welcome a presumably triumphant Bill, leading a suitably chastened Bull, but Bill returns in ignominy, empty-handed. Even more disconcerting is Halsey's statement that the Indians hadn't been trying to escape, but were merely honoring a tribal rite.

This jockeying for position, with the Indians maintaining a lofty and disdainful posture, continues until President Cleveland arrives. The Bull, riding a grey mare, pulls a pistol from his shirt, which scares the bejeezus out of the Presidential party, and fires it into the air to make the mare dance. There is a final confrontation, which takes place during a reception for Cleveland. Bill comes to petition "the Great Father" for his people, but is rebuffed before Cleveland has even heard his requests. Halsey and Bull retreat angrily while Bill praises the President with one of his fatuously nonsensical remarks, "The difference between a President and a chief in a situation like this is

Buffalo Bill attempts to talk to Annie Oakley (Geraldine Chaplin)

the President knows enough to retaliate before it's his turn."

Buffalo Bill comes unglued altogether in a dreamlike, nighttime confrontation with the now-deceased Sitting Bull, who appears and disappears like a curiously solid ghost. Bill lurches around the room at the Mayflower, becoming ever more enmeshed in his own deluded meanderings. He gets deeper and deeper into fantasy, through which a glimmer of truth now and then shines, as when he tells the chief, "I got people with...*no lives*...livin' *through* me! Proud people. My daddy... died without ever seein' me as a star! Tall, profitable...good lookin'...Custer was a good man. He gave the Indians a reason to be famous! Bull, damn you! In a hundred years...I'm still goin' to be Buffalo Bill...star! You're still gonna be The Injun! You wanna stay the same. That's goin'...*backwards*! The difference between

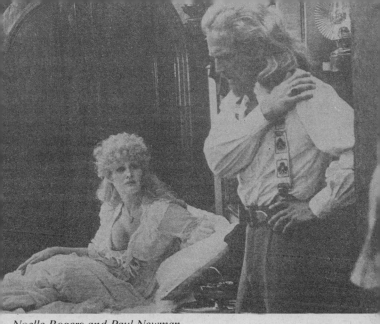

Noelle Rogers and Paul Newman

a white man and a Injun in *all* situations is that a Injun is red! But a Injun is red for a real good reason . . . so we can tell us apart! [Bill looks up at his picture, in which he's riding his proud white stallion, Brigham.] Ain't he ridin' that horse right? Well, if he ain't, how come all of you took him for a king? . . . Truth is whatever gets the loudest applause!"

Bill is like a sad old warrior who has lost his enemies, and with them his reason for living. Now it's all dumb show, endless schoonersful of whiskey. The man who aspires to have "hair as long as Custer's someday" needs a certain amount of contained strife, manageable tension, to keep his fans happy, and to keep himself on his toes. Bill's fantasies dovetail with those of his audience, and Bill and his fans are caught in a mutual delusion. The crowd holds him in awe, and Bill, to continue the life others have wished upon him, must become ever more entangled in a complicated circle of feeding and fulfilling the deceptions he has come to believe are the truth. Bill needs the crowds to ratify his image of himself. As long as they cheer, he's "real," as long as no one pricks the balloon of his infallibility, he's safe from the outside world, a world partly created (after Buntline) by his flacks and sycophants. These are: his producer, Nate Salsbury (Joel Grey), Major Arizona John Burke (Kevin McCarthy), his publicist, and the journalist, Prentiss Ingraham (Allan Nichols). Since Bill and his retinue believe that the stories Buntline spun about Bill's exploits are true, although most of them never happened (The old-timer [Humphrey Gratz] whose tale of *his* discovering Bill as a young man opens and closes the film, believes that *he* is responsible.), Bill has a lot of money and emotional energy tied up in those fables, and he's furious that Buntline is ensconced at the bar libeling his good name behind his back, but too cowardly to tell him off in person. One night, wandering around, and more lonely than he'll admit, Bill finds Buntline and buys him a drink. Now that he's had a last meeting, Buntline is prepared to depart. He tells Bill, "It was the thrill of my life to have invented you." Bill is aghast, shocked by Buntline's saying the unthinkable—a glimpse of the truth has just whispered past him, but Bill can't face it and shrugs off the idea, happy to see his "creator" gallop off to California.

Buntline himself isn't entirely free of his invention, and hymns Bill's praises while slyly chivying at the folk hero who emanated from his own powerful imagination. "No ordinary man would have had the foresight to take credit for acts of bravery and heroism he couldn't have done. And no ordinary man'd realize what tremendous profit could be made by tellin' a pack of lies with witnesses." Buntline realizes that Bill has been caught by the atmosphere of self-congratulation, of dogged refusal on

Buffalo Bill tires to live up to his reputation

everyone's part to face the truth. As Buntline says, "No, Bill Cody can only trust his senses. And when his senses fail, he might just see things as they really are."

But the vested interests of those who make their livings through Bill are against any notion of seeing things as they "really are." Nate Salsbury expresses himself in neologisms close enough to the real words to seem like sense, but sufficiently removed from any authentic meaning to reveal them as nonsense. He tells Buntline, "I'm going to Codyfy the world," and informs a gathering at Bill's table that Bill is "the true monarch of genuity." Nate babbles that paying Bull part of his salary ahead of time is "prevancement," and that Bill, who is expected, will "be out momentably" to greet Sitting Bull and Halsey. Buntline sees through Salsbury's toadying, responding to Nate's "I'm the only partner Bill Cody ever had who told him the truth. And in the end we always agree," with: "I was taught when two partners always agree, one of 'em ain't necessary."

Of course, Salsbury and Major Burke have taken over Buntline's function. Instead of merely writing dime novels about Bill, they are in the very profitable business of manufacturing present-day fables. The slightest hint of news Bill makes, like giving Bull blankets for his people, is grist for Burke's publicity mill, an instant story celebrating Bill's generosity. Burke's flatulent fawning is usually confined to Bill's activities, but he's just as pompous introducing a new opera singer for Bill to conquer as "a compelling cadenza in the cornucopia of classicism." Much later, Burke takes note of another facet of myth-making: "Sitting Bull's not dead. Not as long as Buffalo Bill is alive to kill him in every show!" Burke has absorbed Bill's axiom that truth is whatever gets the most applause.

Ingraham is the third member of the proselytizing

triumvirate surrounding Bill, "the Shakespeare of the half dimes," in Buntline's none-too-flattering phrase. Ingraham aspires to Buntline's former position, spinning praise around yet-to-be-created legends of Bill's renown. And he learns at the feet of the masters, picking up mythifying phraseology from Burke: "I'll even give you the legend: Enemies in '76, friends in '85." Ingraham takes up Buntline's metaphorical speechifying, which he appreciates by noting, in a numbing idiom Salsbury could be proud of: "Every great author has his literisms."

The fourth member of Bill's inner circle is Bill's nephew, Ed Goodman (Harvey Keitel), a not terribly bright young man who makes up in worshipful fervor what he lacks in brains. He protects his uncle from interlopers who threaten to interrupt important conversations, and from Sitting Bull and Halsey when they trespass on his uncle's reception for the President. Ed bars the door, furious at the intrusion, trying to summon the requisite authority to enforce his will. Although young Ed is developing in his job, he hasn't the sophistication to recognize caviar, which he declares is the "funniest lookin' black eyed peas I ever saw," then succumbs to his gauche instincts by spitting out the offending food in disgust.

The clouds lift momentarily on the occasion of Bill's unsuccessful chase, after Sitting Bull's departure for the mountains. Ed comments on the phenomenon of Bill returning empty-handed, saying, "I sure thought you'd catch 'em. They weren't that far ahead." He covers his *faux pas* with, "I don't care what anyone says. God bless Buffalo Bill."

Moments later, as Bill rampages after his current singing innamorata's hated pet bird, brandishing a gun and declaiming, "I hate birds!" Ed, still the dutiful worshipper, echoes, "I hate birds, too."

Of course, the key word in Salsbury's and Burke's lexicon is profits. Their bootlicking serves to keep their star sober enough to stay on his horse and sufficiently content not to make problems. Salsbury and Burke grew wealthy pampering their star; the 1885–86 season grossed over a million dollars and the show played to crowds of up to twenty thousand for five performances a week. In 1886 Bill and most of his troupe journeyed to London to perform in Queen Victoria's Golden Jubilee celebration, an event referred to at the end of the film. Bill asks if Salsbury gave his regards to the Queen when he was in Europe. Salsbury, always eager to pacify his star, replies, "Everybody asked about you." The same scene indicates how successful everyone has become as nephew Ed announces that Buffalo Bill's Wild West should gross over two million dollars that season.

Although the show is several years old at the conclusion of the film, when Sitting Bull's death is announced, things haven't changed much. Major Burke has toned down his flamboyant appearance somewhat, Salsbury is concerned with expanding the business into new areas, and Ed has grown into his job as corporate secretary. He sports a mustache to accentuate the dignity of his mature self. Prentiss Ingraham, looking more and more like his hero, Ned Buntline, is still spinning lucrative fabrications of Buffalo Bill's exploits on the plains.

Buffalo Bill hasn't changed either. He's still downing whiskey by the jugful, rambling to anyone who will listen about his past glory as a Pony Express rider. (And these days, his courtiers are less inclined to listen; they've heard it all before. They make the customary obeisances and go on about their work, which is more important than hearing Bill's windy, ill-remembered half-truths.) He still has his hair touched up to perpetuate the image of the ever-youthful, golden-haired warrior who decimated the buffalo herds and, theoretically, slew Indians by the thousands.

The final scene shows Bill conquering Sitting Bull, now played by William Halsey, raising his knife and Bull's feathered headdress in triumph, his foot planted on a rock as phony as the smile he directs at the cheering crowd. But his eyes waver; he's coming unstuck somewhere between the past, when this *might* have happened, and the present when even he can see, although he refuses to acknowledge it, that he's a fraud. So Buffalo Bill continues radiantly smiling at nothing, a hero for all eternity, as Altman's camera pulls back to show Bill in the center of his self-enclosed world, where nothing can penetrate the solipistic illusion Bill and his retinue thrive on.

For his own reasons, Sitting Bull is as interested in profiting from Buffalo Bill's Wild West show as Bill is in having him perform as an additional attraction—a savage foe to heighten the paying crowd's enthusiasm and their praise for himself. As Ned Buntline observes, "Injuns gear their lives to dreams. And once an Injun dreams, no matter how farfetched it is, he'll wait till he dies for it to come true. White men, they're different. Now, I bring up this dream business 'cause things are startin' to take on an unreal shape. Just think, Sittin' Bull arrives in camp 'cause he's dreamed the President's gonna meet him there. Now Bill can't believe in somebody else's dream 'cause he don't have none of his own. But Sittin' Bull, he never doubted it for one minute. Just put yourself in that Injun's place. You sit in your teepee and you dream. Then you go to wherever your dream might come true, and you wait for real life to catch up. Now, I'm no expert on the subject, but what Bull does is sure a hell of a lot cheaper than mountin' a wild-west show, which is just dreamin' out loud."

When Bull realizes he can't talk to President Cleveland and make him intercede with his people, he leaves, having found that the "Great Father" is great in size only. Altman and Rudolph conceived of Cleveland as a pea-brained oaf who relies on his speechwriter, Fizician (E.L. Doctorow, the author of *Ragtime*, who was pressed into service when he was in Canada discussing the film project with Altman) to prompt him with appropriate remarks for every situation. Fizician helps Cleveland (Pat McCormick) wriggle out of his confrontation with Halsey and Sitting Bull by refusing to hear Bull's request.

Sitting Bull has heeded the call of celebrity and allowed it to bring him where his dream might come true. He knows he must strike a bargain with Bill in order to stay in the show while waiting for Cleveland to arrive, but is unwilling to surrender his dignity in the process. When Bill wants to display Bull as a murdering savage, Halsey counters with an offer to portray Colonel McLaren's slaughter of unarmed Indians at Killdeer Mountain village, a proposal which is obviously unacceptable to Bill and which causes Annie Oakley (Geraldine Chaplin), who sides with Sitting Bull, to threaten to leave the show in support of Bull. Bill pleads with her to stay, and when Annie protests, "But he wants to show the people the truth. Why can't you accept that, just once?" Bill expostulates, "'Cause I got a better sense of history than that!" In order to keep Annie's act, which is important as the show opener, Bill relents: "The little bastard can stay."

Sitting Bull also refuses to reenact, according to Bill's factitious scenario, the death of General Custer. But Bill plans to revenge himself by humbling Sitting Bull in front of an audience. As he tells Halsey, "He's gonna suffer a worse defeat than Custer ever did. Custer could die. Your

Paul Newman and Will Sampson

chief is gonna be humiliated." Bill watches with satisfaction as the crowd, primed by Salsbury's zealous oratory—"...the most feared, the most murderous, the most colorful redskin alive"—boos Sitting Bull's entrance. Sitting Bull, a frail and wizened man, a lone feather stuck in his hair, wearing simple buckskins and a plain wooden cross, enters the arena and rides around on his small pinto. Soon his quiet dignity begins to impress the assemblage, which lapses from catcalls into silence, then raises its collective voice to cheer the unassuming chief. Bill, clad in his gaudy embroidered outfit, is chagrined and enters the ring without looking at his foe.

Sitting Bull triumphs more than once. He parallels Bill's use of murky logic when addressing the President in Sioux while Bill, observing through a curtain, mumbles to a black wrangler (Robert Doqui), "What's he saying?" as though all people whose skins aren't white share a

Sitting Bull (Frank Kaquitts) and his interpreter William Halsey (Will Sampson) confront Buffalo Bill

common language. Cleveland smiles fatuously at Sitting Bull, pretending to understand while querying Fizician. Fizician fakes comprehension. But Sitting Bull's mission is a failure and he decamps. Later, word of his death reaches the camp where, typically, Annie, who weeps openly, is the only one to mourn his passing. The rest are indifferent, concerned only with not upsetting Bill.

Of course, Sitting Bull has to die, if only so that he can become immortal and return to plague Buffalo Bill in his dream-shrouded mental ramblings which pass for philosophical discourse on that stormy night when Bill might have made peace with his past but chose, instead, to bluster his way through. Reality pierces Bill's bewilderment as he observes, "Halsey don't mean a word he says! Which is why he sounds so *real*!" The notion that "truth is whatever gets the loudest applause" is one that Sitting Bull never succumbed to although it has served Bill well over the years.

When it concerns others, Annie Oakley is as concerned with the truth as Halsey and Sitting Bull are, but she's more interested in her unblemished image as a markswoman. She falsifies her "truth" just as Bill does his. Annie waltzes smilingly around the arena, urging the riders who carry her targets to race ever faster, but when she pierces her nervous husband's shoulder, she just as happily pretends that nothing has happened and waltzes herself out of the ring. Missing a complicated shot, she pretends it didn't occur and takes it over, but she's furious and weeps angrily. Her "foremost living target," Annie's husband, Frank Butler (John Considine) is as fallible and human as she is. He's carrying on an affair with one of the laundresses which has resulted in pregnancy, and the laundress chooses the night of the President's reception to give him the good news.

Altman is concerned with the effects of celebrity on the famous, the mutual nourishment derived by the fans and the gods they worship. As he demonstrated in *Nashville*, neither can exist without the other; here the stars of Buffalo Bill's Wild West are the equivalents of that film's country-and-western luminaries, and presumably of movie stars Altman has known. These are all people divorced from the reality of their earlier lives and consequently from any substantive contact with others except the protective sycophants whose livelihood depends on keeping the idol's ego inflated while his feet remain on the ground.

Arthur Kopit says that Buffalo Bill tried to intercede for the Indians, but that his dream of being able to help was unavailing; Altman indicts Bill for not dreaming at all, but both are making larger statements about what people are *able* to dream of, and both conceptions of Buffalo Bill present him as a fool. As Altman himself said, "Can you find somebody who isn't somewhat of a fool?"

3 Women

"This film literally came to me in a dream," says Robert Altman. "And I don't mean that in any mystical sense; I constructed it from that point as a short story and consequently made the film." Altman elaborates further on the circumstances surrounding the creation of *3 Women*: "I needed a film and I also needed to turn down *The Yig Epoxy* [a film Altman had started under David Geffen at Warner Brothers and had decided, for various reasons, was not going to work]. And my wife was sick ... and Shelley Duvall is always in my mind, so it's not difficult, it's not complicated to trace.

"Both girls were in the dream and the title was in the dream. I know Shelley, of course, for years, and I'd been watching all the dailies for the Alan Rudolph film, *Welcome to L.A.*, and Sissy Spacek just wiped me out. I thought she was extraordinary and I was really looking for something for her, so that probably has a lot to do with the idea."

The film Altman "dreamed" concerns Pinky Rose (Sissy Spacek), who is a blank page waiting to be written on. She arrives in Desert Springs, California, with one pair of underpants, a few clothes, and a sewing machine. Pinky meets Millie Lammoreaux (Shelley Duvall) on the first day of her job at the Desert Springs rehabilitation center where Millie walks old folks around a heated pool and explains Pinky's duties to her. Almost immediately Pinky begins filling in the vacancies in her own psyche with attitudes she borrows from Millie. The problem with Pinky's adoration is that Millie is the product of the media. She herself must have been a semicipher when she arrived from Houston (both girls are from Texas), and she has been filling in her own empty spaces with half-understood media messages: She plays Russian roulette with pregnancy, taking the pill "only when I know I'm gonna to do something"; her recipes are catalogued by the length of time they take to cook and are always "melts"—tuna melts, hamburger melts, etc.—or pigs-in-a-blanket. If she couldn't squeeze her food from a tube or open a can, she'd starve. Millie is a self-created media groupie who refers to her flowered yellow, pure Hallmark Cards apartment as "decorated." But she seems to have only partly gotten the messages from the women's magazines, billboards, and television. The rest of her has been left out, and the rest is, of course, her real self. Millie has no "real self," only a collection of attitudes that aren't really hers, except by adoption. She avidly follows men around, hoping for dates and nattering, primarily to herself, as no one pays much attention to her food/colors/hula-lessons conversation, or even notices when she leaves. Millie has the same problems at work, where she may be a responsible therapist but is ignored by her fellow workers who travel in pairs, leaving Millie to team up with Pinky. Pinky quickly becomes Millie's roommate and moves wholeheartedly into Millie's life, slurping beer at "Dodge City" where Millie goes to pick up men. The men there are cops or truck drivers who prefer target practice and dirt-track cycling to Millie's company.

Dodge City is a rundown fake wild-west community

Sissy Spacek and Shelley Duvall pose in front of one of Bodhi Wind's murals for 3 WOMEN

owned by Willie and Edgar Hart (Janice Rule and Robert Fortier) who also own the Purple Sage, the singles apartment complex where Millie lives. The bottoms of the pools at the Desert Springs spa and Purple Sage and a wall at Dodge City are decorated with Willie's frescoes, nightmarish creatures with amphibian/human bodies, long finger nails and tongues, and prominent sexual characteristics, who seem locked in some primordial struggle.

Willie, who is older and pregnant, dresses like a Ukrainian peasant in long dresses with aprons, bandanas, sneakers, and a straw hat, as though she were a misplaced, outdated frontier woman whose frontier consists of Coke, beer, motorcycles, and a neglectful husband. She spends her time painting, plastering herself against her work surface as though she's afraid she'll lose it, gardening, or cleaning Coke bottles out of the pool. She seems to have an active nocturnal life; Willie is nearby whenever something happens. She's almost silent throughout the film, but as played by Rule she is nevertheless a powerful presence.

Edgar is a middle-aged, macho womanizer who used to be Hugh O'Brian's "stunt double." He amuses himself and Pinky with some fancy gun twirling—around Dodge City Edgar wears his gun—and some fakery with a plastic snake and rubber rock. But it's plain that Edgar is scared of growing old. He chases women and pals around with younger men to prove to himself that he isn't. He sucks his gut into his backbone and does what little he can to make time with impressionable girls.

Once Pinky is ensconced with Millie, she works on adopting her life style with a vengeance, telling Millie, "You're the most perfect person I ever met," reading her diary, and taking on Millie's dislike of tomatoes, which

Shelley Duvall and Sissy Spacek at the spa

she heard Millie discussing with one of the old geezers at the Desert Springs center. But if Pinky unconsciously wants to become Millie, there are some minor, shadowy traces of Pinky that are never eradicated, her habitual sloppiness and her ability to spill food and herself all over the place.

At the spa, Millie finds Pinky the smallest bathing suit available, which hangs on Pinky like a shroud. Millie reiterates a line from *McCabe and Mrs. Miller* (the line Julie Christie said to the same actress, Shelley Duvall, who was playing a newly recruited whore), "You're a little like me," as she holds a suit to Pinky's underdeveloped frame. Pinky goes around with the suit pinned up in front, so it won't sag, looking like a lady in maternity clothes who's only one week pregnant.

Pinky disgusts Millie, at Dodge City, by pouring salt into her beer, blowing the foam off onto the counter,

Duvall and Spacek as Millie and Pinky

chugging it down in one gulp, then belching loudly. Pinky leaves her sandals out where Millie can find them and reprove her for her carelessness. During the preparations for Millie's guests ("I'm famous for my dinner parties," she tells Pinky) Pinky spills shrimp cocktail down the front of her dress—to Millie's great distress, as she's bought exactly six cocktails. "Now the table won't be even," she says with consummate annoyance and stomps out to purchase a replacement. This is one of Millie's plastic meals, to which she has invited her ex-roommate, Deidre (Beverly Ross), and some guys. Everything is packaged, poured from a can, or squeezed from an aerosol container. It looks like rancid goo, but Millie is proud of her creations and distraught when her guests callously announce that they aren't coming. Millie stalks out in a huff, declaring, "You don't drink, you don't smoke, you don't do anything you're supposed to do," as

Pinky and Millie at Dodge City

though today's prom queens came with a set of instructions to be ignored at the price of not being popular. She returns later with Edgar, telling Pinky to move onto the rollaway bed in the living room. Pinky obliges but is appalled at Millie's date and wanders out onto the balcony, from which she throws herself into the pool below. Is it despair, a suicide attempt, what? Willie rescues her, calling to the neighbors for help. An ambulance carts Pinky away, and a much chastened Millie, apparently full of guilt, stands vigil outside of Pinky's intensive-care room at the hospital. Millie even refuses a kindly doctor's offer of breakfast, surely a golden opportunity to make time with a likely young man, to stand, her chin wobbling and her eyes filled with tears, watching over Pinky. Millie, with nothing better to do, becomes a self-made martyr, devoting herself to Pinky, who has become a vegetable, a fetus in a coma, kept alive via intravenous tubes. Millie brings her presents and get-well cards, the signatures cudgeled from Millie's uncaring fellow workers at the spa. Millie lies to Pinky, who doesn't hear her, that everyone asks for her, and gives the other girls unheeded bulletins on Pinky's progress. Pinky's accident gives Millie a chance to find her "real self," the semi-nitwit with a generous heart, who can't bear to be hurt, and so pretends she never is, or to see Pinky as an invalid. It's not much of a real self, but for the moment it's all Millie has. Millie has filled in the blanks in her own personality with her loyalty to Pinky.

In desperation, Millie recalls the little Pinky mentioned of her past, and tries to notify Pinky's parents. There is no phone listing, and when she's advised to telegraph, Millie petulantly admits, in what must be a communications breakdown of monumental proportions in her media-dominated life, "But I don't know how to send a telegram." But the Millie who says, "I plan everything," lets nothing stand in her way, and soon she's greeting Mr. and Mrs. Rose (John Cromwell and Ruth Nelson), Pinky's aged parents, who have journeyed from Quitman, Texas, to Desert Springs, bringing their little girl a kitchen motto in a pink-and-white striped bag from the Women's Auxiliary thrift shop. Pinky, on the road to recovery, refuses to acknowledge them as her parents, and has a fit. This is explained as temporary amnesia, and Millie leads Mr. and Mrs. Rose dolefully away. That night she enters their bedroom and finds them quietly making love, clasped in each other's gnarled arms. It's a powerful and tender image, and Millie is totally nonplussed by the scene, as she is by much that involves Pinky.

(Altman explains how director John Cromwell—who did *Of Human Bondage* and *The Prisoner of Zenda*, among many other fine films—and his wife Ruth Nelson came to act in *3 Women*: "Well, Ruth worked in *The Late Show* for us and John was around a lot, and I needed a really elderly couple to play Pinky Rose's parents. John's a terrific actor and a terrific director and a great man. Ninety years old and he'd come over every night after shooting with his Bermuda shorts on and have a drink. All his worry was in the whole film—'I just don't know if it's going to work. If they laugh at us, we're in trouble.' I said, 'Well, if they laugh at us, *I'm* in trouble. I don't think they will.' I've never heard one yet.")

Nonplussed is a term that describes Millie's expression, not only when it's brought on by Pinky's behavior, but whenever she doesn't quite grasp the import of something. Millie is a girl whom things happen *around*, not to, in the ordinary course of events, so dealing with something that affects her directly puts her off and she hasn't the emotional defenses to take it on frontally. Millie is like the girl in high school who was always unpopular no matter how stylish her hair and clothes, how carefully plucked her eyebrows, or how modish her clothes. She's a perennial wallflower, and moving halfway across the country hasn't changed her. A scared little waif peeks out from beneath Millie's bangs, defying the world not to find her fascinating and defying herself to care. Millie circumnavigates situations until she's grasped enough to make them manageable, but by then the event is over and it doesn't matter. In some ways Millie is all raw defenselessness, but in others she has a hide like a buffalo's. In the course of the film, one wonders how many of her neighbors' derisive remarks she hears (girl at poolside to date as Millie sweeps down the stairs in her yellow robe: "Don't look now, but it's thoroughly modern Millie"), and if she hears them, how many register. She seems to move through their midst as though she's under water, and no more reaches her ears than would if she were permanently submerged.

Upon recovery, Pinky is transformed. She insists on being called Mildred, a name she previously detested; instead of merely reading Millie's diary, she writes in it (a) as though she were Millie, and (b) as though it were her own, even going so far as to claim that it is hers and that Millie has no right to read it. She becomes a glamor queen, painting her nails, smoking, and chewing gum, things Millie previously was alone in doing. But more hurtful to Millie than her spite is Pinky's popularity with Millie's single neighbors. Pinky sits by the pool, having driven Millie from their bedroom under the pretense that she'll recuperate faster, and letting Millie support her, more popular than Millie ever dreamed of being. She guzzles juice and plays backgammon, a freckled, pale-blond country mouse transformed by a bump on the head into a with-it city vamp. Once more Millie is nonplussed. Pinky even snares Edgar, who spends at least one afternoon in her bedroom, slurping beer and horsing around, while Pinky coolly evades Millie's questions over the telephone.

But her bliss is interrupted by a disturbing dream, and here Altman's film takes a slightly wrong turning. Pinky dreams of the spa, Millie, her parents, and the pool paintings in negative black and white. It's too heavy-textured, too ominous, too long, and it's a harbinger of an event that happens too soon—that is, immediately. The dream calls attention to itself as a dream, but the rest of the film, which suggests that it too may be a reverie, is more successful in realizing its intentions than the actual dream, which is weighted with too heavy a load of symbolism. A scared Pinky asks Millie if she can share the

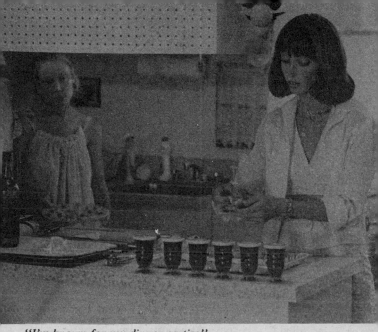

"I'm known for my dinner parties"

bed in the living room with her, and Millie cradles Pinky
protectively in her arms.

Edgar, bragging drunkenly that "Willie is making me
a father," lurches in at that moment and wakes them while
fumbling for a beer. Appalled at his behavior and the fact
that he's left Willie alone, Millie grabs Pinky and tears off
to Dodge City, where they find Willie far gone in labor,
panting and sweaty. Millie orders Pinky to go for a doctor
and helps Willie give birth. This is one of Altman's most
powerful and original scenes. Millie, once again a
Florence Nightingale, keeps up a running line of talk,
asking Willie what to do, kneeling on the bed and letting
Willie put her feet on her shoulders so they can push
against each other. There are repeated shots of Pinky,
immobilized in the yard, fascinated, frightened, and
making no move to get medical help. It's as though seeing
a woman who has a strong identity, that of a potential

mother, is too much for her half-completed personality and she becomes catatonic. The baby is born dead, and as Millie tells Willie, "He's so cold," Willie clasps her boy in her arms while Millie, shaking and covered with Willie's blood, walks into the yard to confront Pinky. She rasps angrily at her for not getting the doctor and slaps Pinky furiously, leaving a streak of blood in Pinky's hair. It isn't beside the point, at this moment, to ask if Willie hurt her baby when she rescued Pinky from the pool, and if this isn't an act for which Pinky atones in the next scene, by regressing into a state of permanently arrested development.

In a film full of compelling and disturbing scenes, it's not surprising to find that the last sequence is both arresting and tranquil, disturbing but reassuring. Pinky, now called Millie, guzzles soda like a teen-ager behind the bar at Dodge City. A boy, delivering Coke, remarks that it was strange how Edgar, who was so good with guns, died. It's left in the air if Edgar was a suicide or died accidentally or if one of the women killed him. Millie II tells the young man she'll get her mom to sign for the order, and Altman pans through the window to Millie I, dressed as a younger version of Willie, gardening as we first saw Willie hoeing the sandy soil. Millie's hair is severely pulled back and she, too, has that weather-touched woman-of-the-West look Willie had. Together Millies I and II walk toward the house, where Willie awakens on the porch, remarks upon the nice dream she just had, and thanks Millie II for offering her some soda. Pinky has given up her attempt to become Millie. It's easier to be someone your own age than to be your own mother, and besides, who would want to?

The dialogue continues as the camera pulls from the house and pans across a heap of junked tires and the

Janice Rule as Willie

scrubby desert. Millie I, sounding like a sleepwalker, tells Millie II to fix some potatoes, and Willie's voice is heard chastising Millie I for being harsh: "I don't know why you have to be so mean to her." We're in the presence of grandmother, mother, and daughter, a complete transformation, but from what? All three women were such lacunae that to claim something has happened to them is to make them carry a larger burden than their fragile characters can support. The ad campaign, seemingly trying to provide a clue, states: "1 woman became 2/2 women became 3/3 women became 1." The reviews for the film were mixed, but leaned toward praise. Altman, speaking to a group of New York film students after a screening at Twentieth Century-Fox, said that Pauline Kael, his long-time champion, hated the film and was not reviewing it for the *New Yorker*. Presumably this is the ultimate kindness, withholding a negative review that would hurt at the box office. But if 3 Women makes money, it will be because of favorable word of mouth, helped by the good reviews. Vincent Canby, writing in *The New York Times*, said: "Someone is bound to ask what it really is about. I'm not sure, but there are a number of possibilities. Since it is the moviemaker's dream more than that of the characters within, it seems to be a consideration of today's women. It's not a narrative in any strict sense, but a contemplation of three stages of a woman's life by a man who appreciates women and may not be without a bit of guilt. It's also about youth and age and (as are all Altman films) about the quality of American life."

Andrew Sarris of the *Village Voice* enthused, "The sustained lyricism of Altman's (and Chuck Rosher's) contemplative and ever-moving camera, the curiously affecting meticulousness of Shelley Duvall's motions and expressions, counterposed with the enchantingly child-like unabashedness of Sissy Spacek's mimicry and emotions, the moody sobriety of Gerald Busby's meditative score, and a spell cast by images that precede and transcend plot and character, all combine to transform potentially profane grotesquerie into sacred ritual. Millie could be written off as a nerd were it not for something magical in Shelley Duvall's performance. Not since Katharine Hepburn's Alice Adams has a female character displayed as much wrongheaded generosity and courage as does Shelley Duvall's Millie.

"He wants his audience above all to remain restless and unsettled. He is the sworn enemy of happy endings and comforting morals."

In the same issue, *Voice* interviewer Cliff Jahr talked to Shelley Duvall about "thoroughly mindless Millie." "I wrote all my own monologues," she says. "Bob would say, 'Why don't you write a monologue just in case we can use it.' And we'd use it. I put a lot of myself in, but I'm not a consumer like Millie. I played her like a Lubitsch comedy—people taking themselves very seriously. It is great fun to watch, as long as it isn't you."

Altman told Howard Kissel of *Women's Wear Daily*, "Since we have to accept everything in reality—which has no logic—and we do, we somehow expect more purpose, more order in our fantasies. Sometimes we want things in our fantasies to be wrapped up in neat packages, which we can't do in our living. But I don't think everyone expects fantasies to be more orderly than reality.

"I think it's about fundamental things. If you strip away our clothes, all the artifacts we've developed, what you're left with is baboons on a rock. The rest is affectation. When the film ends, the three women have killed the man—if they're left on the rock alone, the

Robert Fortier and Sissy Spacek

species ends, which might not be bad.

"I think next year the Oscar nominations for best actress will be Shelley Duvall and Sissy Spacek for *3 Women*, Lily Tomlin for *Late Show* and Geraldine Chaplin for *L.A.* I don't know who the fifth one will be, but she'll win it."

(Altman was reportedly chagrined that his film did not take the best-film award at the 1977 Cannes Festival and that his star, Shelley Duvall, had to share the best-actress award with Monique Mercure.)

Talking about Altman, Michael Murphy recalled a conversation they had early in Murphy's career, in which Altman said he'd like to make a film someday in which two characters enter a hotel. The camera follows one in through a door and follows the second out through another door. Psychologically, *3 Women* is that film. Altman is one of the few directors, perhaps even one of few men, who feel comfortable, or at least somewhat comfortable, with the feminine sides of their natures. Altman can make films in which women are tarnished saviors (*McCabe and Mrs. Miller, Brewster McCloud*) and the men are fools, films in which women are crazy (*That Cold Day in the Park, Images*), but always there is a special appreciation of what women are and what they can do, as opposed to what men are or do, and what makes women unique. Altman's films are not without a certain ambivalence to, not only men's relations with women, but what any sort of involvement with women can lead to. "Get involved with women," Altman's films seem to say, "and it may be wonderful or scary, or both, but you'll never be the same again." His attitude is cautionary, but every time, Altman takes the dare.

A Wedding

Robert Altman's newest project, *A Wedding*, began shooting in June of 1977 as this book was completed. *A Wedding*, with a script by John Considine and Altman, has an enormous cast that includes Lillian Gish, Carol Burnett, Geraldine Chaplin, Nina van Pallandt, Dina Merrill, Desi Arnaz, Jr., Lauren Hutton, Howard Duff, Vittorio Gassman, Mia Farrow, Viveca Lindfors, Gerald Busby, Peggy Ann Garner, Maysie Hoy, Allan Nichols, Pat McCormick, Ruth Nelson, and John Cromwell—many of whom have worked with Altman before.

It deals with a marriage between two cultures, and locations have been set at the Lester Armour estate in Lake Bluff, about forty miles north of Chicago. "The whole film will take place during a large reception given by very wealthy people, the kind of people who travel through Europe and affect accents," Altman says. "Other than funerals, weddings are the last big rituals in our culture. I approve of them both, because they make us all put on ties and shine our shoes."

At a press conference for *3 Women*, Altman talked about *A Wedding* and related an important story about the casting process: "It's going to be a big, big cast, forty-eight major characters, all in one room for the whole movie. So I'm casting for this thing. I gotta be aware that we're going to do this in a couple of hours, that you've got to be able to know something about each person. In casting it, we're looking for things that you, as an audience, will be able to remember—'Oh! That's the guy that his arm was cut off... That's the guy that's short'— whatever it is. And I'm trying to cast the bride. The bride is really very important, because everybody's going to look at the bride and groom; that's what the picture's about, and that's what weddings are about, although they are the least important characters in the wedding, in our culture. I don't know what it is [I'm looking for] because there are no prerequisites—she has to step off the cake.

"[During auditions] this beautiful young girl comes in, and she looks terrific, but she doesn't look any more terrific than the other beautiful young girl... how do I know who's good?... and she smiles and she has braces on her teeth. I said, 'That's the girl. Hire her.'

"Never would I dare hire an actress and then say, 'Let's put braces on her teeth,' and yet the result is the same thing. We've hired a girl who has braces, but there's something about the fact that there is the truth, to me, and to her, in the fact that those braces are there, that makes it okay. Those delineations *are* that serious. I feel very comfortable in doing that if I know it's true. If I'm manufacturing it for some reason, then it doesn't work."

* * *

Robert Altman has succeeded in his proclaimed goal of creating difficult films that demand an emotional response, rather than an intellectual one, from the audience. As he says, "I don't create any worlds, those people arc there all the time. Every time you learn something, every moment you pass, you're solidifying your own character, but you're also dying. And there's nothing wrong with that."

Altman sounds deceptively off hand and casual as he dismisses the films he works so hard to create: "I really have nothing to say to anybody. I have no philosophy. All I'm trying to do is paint a picture and show it to you. It's like a sand castle. It's going to go away."

Filmography

Bodyguard

Producer	Sid Rogell
Director	Richard Fleischer
Screenplay	Fred Niblo, Jr., and Harry Essex, based on a story by George W. George and Robert Altman
Cinematographer	Robert de Grasse
Music	Paul Sawtell
Musical Director	C. Bakaleinikoff
Editor	Elmo Williams
Art Directors	Albert S. D'Agostino and Field Gray
Sound	Earl A. Wolcott and Terry Kellum
Sets	Darrel Silvera and James Altwies
Special Effects	Russell A. Cully
Distributor	RKO Radio Pictures, Inc.
Release Date	1948
Running Time	62 Minutes

Cast

Mike Carter	Lawrence Tierney
Doris Brewster	Priscilla Lane
Freddie Dysen	Philip Reed
Connie	June Clayworth
Gene Dysen	Elisabeth Risdon
Fenton	Steve Brodie
Lieutenant Borden	Frank Fenton
Captain Wayne	Charles Cane

The Delinquents

Producer	Robert Altman
Screenplay	Robert Altman
Cinematographer	Charles Paddock
Music	Bill Nolan Quintet Minus Two
	Song, "The Dirty Rock Boogie," by Bill Nolan and Ronnie Norman, sung by Julia Lee
Editor	Helene Turner
Art Director	Chet Allen
Assistant Director	Reza Badiyi
Sound	Bob Post
Sound Effects	Fred Brown
Camera Operator	Harry Birch
Production Manager	Joan Altman
Distributor	United Artists
Release Date	1957
Running Time	75 minutes

Cast

Scotty	Tom Laughlin
Cholly	Peter Miller
Eddy	Richard Bakalyan
Janice	Rosemary Howard
Mrs. White	Helene Hawley
Mr. White	Leonard Belove
Mrs. Wilson	Lotus Corelli
Mr. Wilson	James Lantz
Sissy	Christine Altman
Jay	George Kuhn
Meg	Pat Stedman
Chizzy	Norman Zands
Steve	James Leria
Molly	Jet Pinkston
Bartender	Kermit Echols
Station Attendant	Joe Adleman

The James Dean Story

Producers, Directors, and Editors	George W. George and Robert Altman
Screenplay	Stewart Stern
Music	Leith Stevens
Production Designer	Louis Clyde Stoumen
Titles Designed By	Maurice Binder
Title Illustrations	David Stone Martin
Sound	Cathey Burrow
Sound Designers	Bert Schoenfeld, James Nelson and Jack Kirschner
Still Sequences Designed By	Camera Eye Pictures, Inc.

Theme Song, "Let Me Be Loved"	Jay Livingston and Ray Evans, sung by Tommy Sands
Assistant to the Producers	Louis Lombardo
Narration	Martin Gabel
Distributor	Warner Brothers
Release Date	1957
Running Time	82 Minutes

Contributing Photographers: Dennis Stock, Roy Schatt, Frank Worth, Weegee, Edward Martin, Dick Miller, Peter Basch, Carlyle Blackwell, Jr., Tom Caffrey, Jack Delano, Murray Garrett, Paul Gilliam, Globe Photos, Inc., Fred Jordan, Impact Photos, Inc., Louis Lombardo, Magnum Photos, Inc., Russ Meyer, Don Ornitz, Paul Popesil, Charles Robinson, Jack Stager, Phil Stern, Louis Clyde Stoumen, William Veercamp, Wide World Photos, Inc., UCLA Theatre Arts, California Highway Patrol.

Countdown

Screenplay	Loring Mandel, based on the novel *The Pilgrim Project*, by Hank Searls
Executive Producer	William Conrad
Cinematographer	William W. Spencer
Music	Leonard Rosenman
Editor	Gene Milford
Art Director	Jack Poplin
Assistant Director	Victor Vallejo
Sound	Everett A. Hughes
Unit Manager	J. Russell Llewellyn
Makeup	Gordon Bau
Hair Stylist	Jean Burt Reilly

Dialogue Supervisor	Stacy Harris
Sets	Ralph S. Hurst
Distributor	Warner Brothers
Release Date	1968
Processes	Technicolor, Panavision
Running Time	101 Minutes

Cast

Lee Stegler	James Caan
Chiz	Robert Duvall
Mickey	Joanna Moore
Jean	Barbara Baxley
Gus	Charles Aidman
Ross	Steve Ihnat
Rick	Michael Murphy
Larson	Ted Knight
Ehrman	Stephen Coit
Dunc	John Rayner
Seidel	Charles Irving
Stevie	Bobby Riha, Jr.

That Cold Day in the Park

Producers	Donald Factor and Leon Mirell
Screenplay	Gillian Freeman, from the novel by Richard Miles
Cinematographer	Laszlo Kovacs
Music	Johnny Mandel
Editor	Danford B. Greene
Art Director	Leon Ericksen

Associate Producer	Robert Eggenweiler
Assistant Director	Harold Schneider
Second Assistant Director	Graeme Clifford
Sound	John Gusselle
Production Manager	James Margellos
Distributor	Commonwealth United Entertainment, Inc.
Release Date	1969
Process	Eastman Color
Running Time	110 Minutes

Cast

Frances Austen	Sandy Dennis
The Boy	Michael Burns
Nina	Suzanne Benton
Nick	John Garfield, Jr.
Sylvia	Luana Anders
The Rounder	Michael Murphy
Dr. Stevenson	Edward Greenhalgh
Mrs. Ebury	Doris Buckingham
Mr. Ebury	Frank Wade
Mrs. Pitt	Alicia Ammon
Mr. Pitt	Lloyd Berry
The Prostitute	Linda Sorensen
Mrs. Parnell	Rae Brown

M*A*S*H

Producer	Ingo Preminger
Screenplay	Ring Lardner, Jr., based on the novel by Richard Hooker

Cinematographer	Harold E. Stine
Music	Johnny Mandel
Song, "Suicide Is Painless"	Lyrics by Mike Altman, music by Johnny Mandel
Editor	Danford B. Greene
Art Directors	Jack Martin Smith and Arthur Lonergan
Associate Producer	Leon Ericksen
Assistant Director	Ray Taylor, Jr.
Assistant to the Producer	Y. Ross Levy
Sound	Bernard Freericks and John Stack
Orchestration	Herbert Spencer
Title Theme	Music Performed By Ahmad Jamal
Makeup Supervisor	Dan Striepeke
Makeup Artist	Lester Berns
Hair Stylist	Edith Lindon
Medical Advisor	Dr. David Sachs
Unit Production Manager	Norman A. Cook
Title Design	Pacific Title and Art Studio
Set Decoration	Walter M. Scott and Stuart A. Reiss
Special Effects	L. B. Abbott and Art Cruickshank
Distributor	Twentieth Century-Fox
Release Date	1969
Processes	Color by DeLuxe, Panavision
Running Time	116 Minutes

Cast

Capt. "Hawkeye" Pierce	Donald Sutherland
Capt. "Trapper" John McIntyre	Elliott Gould

Capt. "Duke" Forrest	Tom Skerritt
Major Margaret "Hot Lips" Houlihan	Sally Kellerman
Major Frank Burns	Robert Duvall
Lt. Dish	Jo Ann Pflug
Father "Dago Red" Mulcahy	René Auberjonois
Col. Henry Blake	Roger Bowen
Cpl. Radar O'Reilly	Gary Burghoff
Sgt. Major Vollmer	David Arkin
Capt. Oliver Wendell "Spearchucker" Jones	Fred Williamson
Capt. "Me Lay" Marston	Michael Murphy
Ho-Jon	Kim Atwood
Cpl. Judson	Tim Brown
Lt. Leslie	Indus Arthur
Capt. Walt Waldowski, the "Painless Pole"	John Schuck
Pfc. Seidman	Ken Prymus
Capt. Scorch	Dawne Damon
Ugly John	Carl Gottlieb
Capt. "Knocko" McCarthy	Tamara Horrocks
Gen. Hammond	G. Wood
Sgt. Gorman	Bobby Troup
Pvt. Warren Boone	Bud Cort
Capt. Murrhardt	Danny Goldman
Capt. Bandini	Corey Fischer
Col. Wallace C. Merrill	J. B. Douglas
Japanese Servant	Yoko Young

Football Players: Ben Davidson, Fran Tarkenton, Howard Williams, Jack Concannon, John Myers, Tom Woodeschick, Tommy Brown, Buck Buchanan, Nolan Smith

Brewster McCloud

Producer	Lou Adler
Screenplay	Doran William Cannon
Assistant to the Producer	Ross Levy
Cinematographers	Jordan Cronenweth and Lamar Boren
Music	Gene Page
Editor and Second Unit Director	Lou Lombardo
Wings Designed by	Leon Ericksen
Art Directors	George W. Davis and Preston Ames
Associate Producers	Robert Eggenweiler and James Margellos
Assistant Director	Tommy Thompson
Sound	Harry W. Tetrick and William McCaughey
Makeup	Edwin Butterworth
Hair Stylist	Dorothy White
Casting	Gary Wayne Chason
Distributor	Metro-Goldwyn-Mayer, Inc.
Release Date	1970
Processes	Metrocolor, Panavision
Running Time	104 Minutes

Cast

Brewster McCloud	Bud Cort
Louise	Sally Kellerman
Shaft	Michael Murphy
Weeks	William Windom
Suzanne	Shelley Duvall

The Lecturer	René Auberjonois
Abraham Wright	Stacy Keach
Johnson	John Schuck
Daphne Heap	Margaret Hamilton
Hope	Jennifer Salt
Hines	Corey Fischer
Crandall	G. Wood
Douglas Breen	Bert Remsen
Bernard	William Baldwin
Band Conductor	William Henry Bennet
Camera Store Clerk	Gary Wayne Chason
Butler	Ellis Gilbert
Manager, Feathered Nest Sanatorium	Verdie Henshaw
Assistant Manager, Camera Store	Robert Warner
Professor Aggnout	Keith V. Erickson
Color Lab Man	Thomas Danko
Police Chaplain	W. E. Terry, Jr.
Wendel	Ronnie Cammack
Manager, Tanninger's Nursing Home	Dixie M. Taylor
Nursing Home Attendant	Pearl Coffey Chason
Nursing Home Manageress	Amelia Parker

Songs written by John Phillips. "Last of the Unnatural Acts," "White Feather Wings," "The First and Last Thing You Do," "I Promise Not to Tell," composed by Rosamund Johnson. "Lift Every Voice and Sing," composed by James Weldon Johnson. "Last of the Unnatural Acts," "The First and Last Thing You Do," "I Promise Not to Tell," sung by John Phillips. "Lift Every Voice and Sing," "White Feather Wings," sung by Merry Clayton.

McCabe and Mrs. Miller

Producers	David Foster and Mitchell Brower
Screenplay	Robert Altman and Brian McKay, based on the novel *McCabe* by Edmund Naughton
Cinematographer	Vilmos Zsigmond
Songs	Leonard Cohen
Fiddler	Brantley F. Kearns
Editor and Second Unit Director	Louis Lombardo
Production Designer	Leon Ericksen
Art Directors	Philip Thomas and Al Locatelli
Associate Producer	Robert Eggenweiler
Assistant Director	Tommy Thompson
Second Assistant Director	Irby Smith
Sound	John V. Gusselle and William A. Thompson
Continuity	Joan Maguire
Makeup	Robert Jiras, Ed Butterworth, and Phyllis Newman
Hair Stylist	Barry Richardson
Wardrobe	Ilse Richter
Unit Production Manager	James Margellos
Second Unit Photography	Rod Parkhurst
Casting	Graeme Clifford
Sound Mixer	Barry P. Jones
Property Master	Syd Greenwood
Title Design	Anthony Goldschmidt
Special Effects	Marcel Vercoutere
Distributor	Warner Brothers
Release Date	1970

Processes	Technicolor, Panavision
Running Time	121 Minutes

Cast

John Q. McCabe	Warren Beatty
Mrs. Miller (Constance)	Julie Christie
Patrick Sheehan	René Auberjonois
Dog Butler	Hugh Millais
Ida Coyl	Shelley Duvall
Eugene Sears	Michael Murphy
Smalley	John Schuck
Mr. Elliott, the Preacher	Corey Fischer
Clement Samuels, the Lawyer	William Devane
Ernie Hollander	Anthony Holland
Bart Coyl	Bert Remsen
Cowboy	Keith Carradine
Breed	Jace Vander Veen
Kid	Manfred Shulz
Lily	Jackie Crossland
Kate	Elizabeth Murphy
Blanche	Linda Sorenson
Birdie	Elizabeth Knight
Maysie	Maysie Hoy
Ruth	Linda Kupecek
Eunice	Janet Wright
Alma	Carey Lee McKenzie
Archer	Tom Hill
Jeremy Berg	Jeremy Newsom
Sheehan's Bartender	Wayne Robson
Riley Quinn	Jack Riley
Town Drunk	Robert Fortier

McCabe's Bartender	Wayne Grace
Shorty Dunn	Wesley Taylor
Mrs. Dunn	Anne Cameron
Bill Cubbs	Graeme Campbell
J.J.	J. S. Johnson
Joe Shortreed	Joe Clarke
Andy Anderson	Harry Trader
Gilchrist	Edwin Collier
Quigley	Terence Kelly
Fiddler	Brantley F. Kearns
Buffalo	Don Francks
Sumner Washington	Rodney Gage
Mrs. Washington	Lili Francks

Joan McGuire, Harvey Lowe, Eric Schneider, Milos Zalovic, Claudine Melgrave, Derek Deurvorst, Alexander Diakun, Gordon Robertson

Images

Producer	Tommy Thompson
Screenplay	Robert Altman
Cinematographer	Vilmos Zsigmond
Music	John Williams
Editor	Graeme Clifford
Production Designer	Leon Ericksen
Assistant to the Producer	Jean d'Oncieu
Assistant Director	Seamus Byrne
Sound Recordist	Liam Saurin
Sounds	Stomu Yamash'ta
Dubbing Mixer	Doug Turner
Boom Operator	Noel Quinn

Gaffer	Jack Conroy
Continuity	Joan Bennett
Makeup	Toni Delaney
Hair Stylist	Barry Richardson
Wardrobe	Jack Gallagher
Miss York's Clothes	Raymond Ray
Grip	Paddy Keogh
Production Manager	Sheila Collins
Camera Assistants	Earl Clark and Nico Vermuelin
Assistant Editors	Michael Kelliher, David Spiers, and Robin Buick
Sound Editor	Rodney Holland
Distributor	Columbia Pictures (A Lion's Gate-Hemdale Group Production)
Release Date	1972
Running Time	101 Minutes

Cast

Cathryn	Susannah York
Hugh	René Auberjonois
René	Marcel Bozzuffi
Marcel	Hugh Millais
Susannah	Cathryn Harrison
Neighbor	John Morley

The Long Goodbye

Producer	Jerry Bick
Screenplay	Leigh Brackett, based on the novel by Raymond Chandler

Executive Producer	Elliot Kastner
Cinematographer	Vilmos Zsigmond
Music	John Williams
Title Song	Johnny Mercer and John Williams; played by Dave Grusin Trio
Editor	Lou Lombardo
Associate Producer	Robert Eggenweiler
Assistant Director	Tommy Thompson
Sound	John V. Speak
Gaffer	Randy Glass
Script Supervisor	Adele Bravos
Makeup	Bill Miller
Hair Stylist	Lynda Gurasich
Wardrobe (Male)	Kent James
(Female)	Marjorie Wahl
Key Grip	Ken Adams
Distributor	United Artists
Release Date	1973
Processes	Technicolor, Panavision
Running Time	112 Minutes

Cast

Philip Marlowe	Elliott Gould
Eileen Wade	Nina van Pallandt
Roger Wade	Sterling Hayden
Marty Augustine	Mark Rydell
Dr. Verringer	Henry Gibson
Harry	David Arkin
Terry Lennox	Jim Bouton
Morgan	Warren Berlinger
Jo Ann Eggenweiler	Jo Ann Brody
Hood	Jack Knight

Pepe	Pepe Callahan
Hood	Vince Palmieri
Hood	Arnold Strong
Muscle Man	Arnold Schwarzenegger
Marlowe's Neighbor	Rutanya Alda
Marlowe's Neighbor	Tammy Shaw
Piano Player	Jack Riley
Colony Guard	Ken Sansom
Bartender	Danny Goldman
Real Estate Lady	Sybil Scotford
Detective Farmer	Steve Coit
Detective	Tracy Harris
Detective Green	Jerry Jones
Clerk	Rodney Moss
Nurse	Kate Murtagh

Thieves Like Us

Screenplay	Calder Willingham, Joan Tewkesbury, and Robert Altman, based on Edward Anderson's novel
Executive Producer	George Litto
Cinematographer	Jean Boffety
Editor	Lou Lombardo
Visual Consultant	Jack DeGovia
Assistant Visual Consultant	Scott Bushnell
Associate Producers	Robert Eggenweiler and Thomas Hal Philips
Assistant Director	Tommy Thompson
Second Assistant Director	Mike Kusley
Sound Mixer	Don Matthews

Camera Crew	George Bouillet, James Blandford, and Harry Walsh III
Property Master	Marty Wunderlich
Cars	Paul Neanover
	Jean D'Oncieu
Grips	Eddie Lara, Dennis Kuneff, and Billy Record
	Cinemobile Systems
Assistant Editors	Tony Lombardo and Dennis Hill
Dubbing Mixer	Richard Voriseck
Radio Research	John Dunning
Research Historian	Carol Gister
Distributor	United Artists
Release Date	1974
Process	DeLuxe Color
Running Time	123 Minutes

Cast

Bowie	Keith Carradine
Keechie Mobley	Shelley Duvall
Elmo (Chicamaw) Mobley	John Schuck
T-Dub Masefield	Bert Remsen
Mattie	Louise Fletcher
Lula	Ann Latham
Dee Mobley	Tom Skerritt
Captain Stammers	Al Scott
Jasbo	John Roper
Noel Joy	Mary Waits
James Mattingly	Rodney Lee, Jr.

Alvin	William Watters
Lady in Train Station	Joan Tewkesbury
Bank Hostage	Dr. Edward Fisher
Bank Hostage	Josephine Bennett
Bank Hostage	Howard Warner
Woman in Accident	Eleanor Mathews
Coca-Cola Girl	Pam Warner
Sheriff	Walter Cooper
Sheriff	Lloyd Jones

California Split

Producers	Robert Altman and Joseph Walsh
Screenplay	Joseph Walsh
Executive Producers	Aaron Spelling and Leonard Goldberg
Cinematographer	Paul Lohmann
Music Played and Sung by	Phyllis Shotwell
Editor	Lou Lombardo
Art Director	Leon Ericksen
Associate Producer	Robert Eggenweiler
Assistant Director	Tommy Thompson
Second Assistant Director	Alan Rudolph
Sound Mixer	Jim Webb
Dubbing Mixer	Richard Fortman
Camera Operator	Edward Koons
Assistants	Richard Colean and Ron Frantzvog
Gaffer	Randy Glass
Sound Crew	Chris McLaughlin and George Wycoff

Script Supervisor	Carole Gister
Production Coordinator	Kelly Marshall
Makeup	Joe di Bella
Wardrobe	Hugh McFarland
Grips	Harry Rez, Tom Doherty, and Eddie Lara
Casting	Scott Bushnell
Assistant Editors	Tony Lombardo and Dennis Hill
Sound Editor	Kay Rose (Lion's Gate 8-Track Sound Services)
Assistant	Randy Kelley
Set Decorator	Sam Jones
Property Master	Jerry Graham
Editorial Assistants	Marion Segal and Stephen W. Altman
Assistant to the Producers	Jac Cashin
Title Design	Dan Perri
Title Editor	O. Nicholas Brown
Distributor	Columbia Pictures
Release Date	1974
Processes	Color, Panavision
Running Time	111 Minutes

Cast

Bill Denny	George Segal
Charlie Waters	Elliott Gould
Barbara Miller	Ann Prentiss
Susan Peters	Gwen Welles
Lew	Edward Walsh
Sparkie	Joseph Walsh
Helen Brown	Bert Remsen

Lady on the Bus	Barbara London
Reno Barmaid	Barbara Ruick
Robber	Jay Fletcher
Lloyd Harris	Jeff Goldblum
Receptionist	Barbara Colby
First Bartender	Vince Palmieri
Go-Go Girl	Alyce Passman
Mother	Joanne Strauss
Second Bartender	Jack Riley
Woman at Bar	Sierra Bandit
Man at Bar	John Considine
Harvey	Eugene Troobnick
Used Car Salesman	Richard Kennedy
Tenor	John Winston
Kenny	Bill Duffy
Reno Dealer	Mike Greene
Nugie	Tom Signorelli
Nugie's Wife	Sharon Compton
California Club Poker Players	Arnold Herzstein, Marc Cavell, Alvin Weissman, Mickey Fox, and Carol Lohmann
Reno Poker Players	"Amarillo Slim" Preston, Winston Lee, Harry Drackett, Thomas Hal Phillips, Ted Say, and A. J. Hood
Most of the Other Players, from Synanon	

Nashville

Producer	Robert Altman
Screenplay	Joan Tewkesbury
Executive Producers	Martin Starger and Jerry Weintraub
Cinematographer	Paul Lohmann
Music Arranged and Supervised By	Richard Baskin
Editors	Sidney Levin and Dennis Hill
Associate Producers	Robert Eggenweiler and Scott Bushnell
Assistant Directors	Tommy Thompson and Alan Rudolph
Sound	Jim Webb and Chris McLaughlin
Camera Operator	Edward Koons
Gaffers	Randy Glass and Mike Marlett
Script Supervisor	Joyce King
Makeup	Tommy Thompson
Hair Stylist	Ann Wadlington
Wardrobe	Jules Melillo
Grips	Harry Pez and Eddie Lara
Casting (Local)	Joann Doster
Assistant Editors	Tony Lombardo and Tom Walls
Sound Editor	William A. Sawyer
Assistant	Randy Kelley
Property Master	Bob Anderson
Political Campaign	Thomas Hal Phillips
Production Coordinator	Kelly Marshall
Assistant to the Producer	Jac Cashin
Sound System	Lion's Gate 8-Track Sound
Rerecording Mixer	Richard Portman

Music Recorded By	Gene Eichelberger and Johnny Rosen
Production Assistants	Angel Dominquez, Ron Hecht, Steve Altman, Mark Eggenweiler, Maysie Hoy, Allan Highfill, Roger Frappier
Title Design	Dan Perri
Production Secretary	Elaine Bradish
Distributor	Paramount Pictures Corp.
Release Date	1975
Running Time	159 Minutes

Cast

Norman	David Arkin
Lady Pearl	Barbara Baxley
Delbert Reese	Ned Beatty
Connie White	Karen Black
Barbara Jean	Ronee Blakley
Tommy Brown	Timothy Brown
Tom Frank	Keith Carradine
Opal	Geraldine Chaplin
Wade	Robert Doqui
L.A. Joan	Shelley Duvall
Barnett	Allen Garfield
Haven Hamilton	Henry Gibson
Pfc. Glenn Kelly	Scott Glenn
Tricycle Man	Jeff Goldblum
Albuquerque	Barbara Harris
Kenny Fraiser	David Hayward
John Triplette	Michael Murphy
Bill	Allan Nichols
Bud Hamilton	Dave Peel

Mary	Christina Raines
Star	Bert Remsen
Linnea Reese	Lily Tomlin
Sueleen Gay	Gwen Welles
Mr. Green	Keenan Wynn

Featuring

Jimmy Reese	James Dan Calvert
Donna Reese	Donna Denton
Trout	Merle Kilgore
Jewel	Carol McGinnis
Smokey Mountain Laurel	Sheila Bailey
Frog	Richard Baskin
Themselves	Jonnie Barnett, Vassar Clements, Misty Mountain Boys, Sue Barton, Patti Bryant, Elliott Gould, Julie Christie

Songs

"200 Years"	Lyrics by Henry Gibson, Music by Richard Baskin
"Yes, I Do"	Lyrics and Music by Richard Baskin and Lily Tomlin
"Down to the River"	Lyrics and Music by Ronee Blakley
"Let Me Be the One"	Lyrics and Music by Richard Baskin

"Sing a Song"	Lyrics and Music by Joe Raposo
"The Heart of a Gentle Woman"	Lyrics and Music by Dave Peel
"Bluebird"	Lyrics and Music by Ronee Blakley
"The Day I Looked Jesus in the Eye"	Lyrics and Music by Richard Baskin and Robert Altman
"Memphis"	Lyrics and Music by Karen Black
"I Don't Know If I Found It in You"	Lyrics and Music by Karen Black
"For the Sake of the Children"	Lyrics and Music by Richard Baskin and Richard Reicheg
"Keep a' Goin'"	Lyrics by Henry Gibson, Music by Richard Baskin and Henry Gibson
"Swing Low Sweet Chariot"	Arrangements by Millie Clements
"Rolling Stone"	Lyrics and Music by Karen Black
"Honey"	Lyrics and Music by Keith Carradine
"Tapedeck in His Tractor (The Cowboy Song)"	Lyrics and Music by Ronee Blakley
"Dues"	Lyrics and Music by Ronee Blakley
"I Never Get Enough"	Lyrics and Music by Richard Baskin and Ben Raleigh
"Rose's Café"	Lyrics and Music by Allan Nichols

"Old Man Mississippi"	Lyrics and Music by Juan Grizzle
"My Baby's Cookin' in Another Man's Pan"	Lyrics and Music by Jonnie Barnett
"One, I Love You"	Lyrics and Music by Richard Baskin
"I'm Easy"	Lyrics and Music by Keith Carradine
"It Don't Worry Me"	Lyrics and Music by Keith Carradine
"Since You've Gone"	Lyrics and Music by Gary Busey
"Trouble in the U.S.A."	Lyrics and Music by Arlene Barnett
"My Idaho Home"	Lyrics and Music by Ronee Blakley

Buffalo Bill and the Indians, Or, Sitting Bull's History Lesson

Producer	Robert Altman
Screenplay	Alan Rudolph and Robert Altman, based on the play, *Indians*, by Arthur Kopit
Executive Producer	David Susskind
Production Executive	Tommy Thompson
Cinematographer	Paul Lohmann
Production Designer	Tony Masters
Music	Richard Baskin
Editors	Peter Appleton and Dennis Hill
Art Director	Jack Maxsted

Associate Producers	Robert Eggenweiler, Scott Bushnell, and Jac Cashin
Assistant Director	Tommy Thompson
Second Assistant Director	Rob Lockwood
Sound	Jim Webb and Chris McLaughlin
Sound System	Lion's Gate 8-Track Sound
Camera Operators	Eddie Koons and Jack Richards
Gaffer	J. Michael Marlett
Titan Boom	Norman Walke
Script Supervisor	John Binder
Unit Manager	Les Kimber
Makeup	Monty Westmore
Scenic Artist	Rusty Cox
Costume Designer	Anthony Powell
Wardrobe	Jules Melillo
Costume Assistant	Allen Highfill
Grip	Art Brooker
Assistant Editors	Tony Lombardo, Tom Walls, and Mark Eggenweiler
Apprentice Editor	Steve Altman
Set Decorator and Property Master	Denny Parrish
Assistant	Graham Sumner
Sound Editor	Richard Oswald
Re-recording Mixer	Richard Portman
Special Effects	Joe Zomar, Logan Frazee, Bill Zomar, Terry Frazee, and John Thomas
Head Wrangler	John Scott

Steam Engines and Other Units on Loan From	Reynolds Museum, Wetaskiwin, Alberta, Canada
Location	Stoney Indian Reserve, Alberta, Canada
Presented By	Dino De Laurentiis
Distributor	United Artists
Release Date	1976
Processes	Color, Panavision
Running Time	123 Minutes

Cast

The Star, William F. Cody, "Buffalo Bill"	Paul Newman
The Producer, Nate Salsbury	Joel Grey
The Publicist, Major Arizona John Burke	Kevin McCarthy
The Relative, Ed Goodman	Harvey Keitel
The Journalist, Colonel Prentiss Ingraham	Allan Nichols
The Sure Shot, Annie Oakley	Geraldine Chaplin
The Sure Shot's Manager	John Considine
The Wrangler, Osborne Dart	Robert Doqui
The Treasurer, Jules Keen	Mike Kaplan
The Bartender, Crutch	Bert Remsen
The Mezzo-Contralto, Margaret	Bonnie Leaders
The Lyric-Coloratura, Lucille Du Charmes	Noelle Rogers

The Lyric-Soprano, Nina Cavalini	Evelyn Lear
The Indian Agent, McLaughlin	Denver Pyle
The Indian, Chief Sitting Bull	Frank Kaquitts
The Interpreter, William Halsey	Will Sampson
The Arenic Director, Johnny Baker	Ken Krossa
The King of the Cowboys, Buck Taylor	Fred N. Larsen
The Cowboy Trick Riders	Jerry and Joy Duce
The Mexican Whip and Fast Draw Act, Munoz and Manuel	Alex Green and Gary MacKenzie
The Old Soldier	Humphrey Gratz
The President of the United States, Grover Cleveland	Pat McCormick
The First Lady, Frances Folsom Cleveland	Shelley Duvall
The Speech Writer, O. W. Fizician	E. L. Doctorow
The Legend Maker, Ned Buntline	Burt Lancaster
The Horse, Brigham	Pluto Calcedona, loaned by Raflyn Farms, Snohomish, Washington

Brave Cowboys and Fierce Indians played by Fierce Indians and Brave Cowboys from the Stoney Indian Reserve and the Calgary Stampede

3 Women

Producer	Robert Altman
Screenplay	Robert Altman
Cinematographer	Chuck Rosher
Music	Gerald Busby
Editor	Dennis Hill
Visual Consultant	J. Allen Highfill
Art Director	James D. Vance
Associate Producers	Robert Eggenweiler and Scott Bushnell
Second Assistant Director	Carol Himes
Sound	Jim Webb and Chris McLaughlin
Rerecording Mixer	Richard Portman
Camera Operator	John Bailey
Postproduction Supervisor	Bill Sawyer
Gaffer	Tim Evans
Postproduction	Westwood Editorial
Music Editor	Tom Walls
Makeup	Monty Westmore
Hair Stylist	Kaye Downall
Wardrobe	Jules Melillo
Best Boy	John Garcia
Grip	Harry Rez
Best Boy Grip	Jacque L. Wallace
Murals	Bodhi Wind
Dolly Grip	Robert L. Bennett
Assistant Editors	Tony Lombardo, Mark Eggenweiler, and Maisie Hoy
Sound Editors	David M. Horton and Bill Phillips
Sets	Patricia Resnick

Title Design	Dan Perri
First Camera Assistant	Robert E. Dawes, Jr.
Second Camera Assistant	Glenn Shimada
Distributor	Twentieth Century-Fox
Processes	DeLuxe Color, Panavision
Running Time	125 Minutes

Cast

Millie Lammoreaux	Shelley Duvall
Pinky Rose	Sissy Spacek
Willie Hart	Janice Rule
Edgar Hart	Robert Fortier
Mrs. Rose	Ruth Nelson
Mr. Rose	John Cromwell
Ms. Bunweill	Sierra Pecheur
Dr. Maas	Craig Richard Nelson
Doris	Maysie Hoy
Alcira	Belita Moreno
Polly	Leslie Ann Hudson
Peggy	Patricia Ann Hudson
Deidre	Beverly Ross
Dr. Norton	John Davey

ALL TIME BESTSELLERS
FROM POPULAR LIBRARY

☐	THE BERLIN CONNECTION—Simmel	08607-6	1.95
☐	THE BEST PEOPLE—Van Slyke	08456-1	1.95
☐	A BRIDGE TOO FAR—Ryan	08373-5	2.50
☐	THE CAESAR CODE—Simmel	08413-8	1.95
☐	DO BLACK PATENT LEATHER SHOES REALLY REFLECT UP?—Powers	08490-1	1.75
☐	ELIZABETH—Hamilton	04013-0	1.75
☐	THE FURY—Farris	08620-3	2.25
☐	THE HAB THEORY—Eckert	08597-5	2.50
☐	HARDACRE—Skelton	04026-2	2.25
☐	THE HEART LISTENS—Van Slyke	08520-7	1.95
☐	TO KILL A MOCKINGBIRD—Lee	08376-X	1.75
☐	THE LAST BATTLE—Ryan	08381-6	2.25
☐	THE LAST CATHOLIC IN AMERICA—Powers	08523-2	1.50
☐	THE LONGEST DAY—Ryan	08380-8	1.95
☐	LOVE'S WILD DESIRE—Blake	08616-5	1.95
☐	THE MIXED BLESSING—Van Slyke	08491-X	1.95
☐	MORWENNA—Goring	08604-1	1.95
☐	THE RICH AND THE RIGHTEOUS —Van Slyke	08585-1	1.95

Buy them at your local bookstores or use this handy coupon for ordering:

Popular Library, P.O. Box C730, 524 Myrtle Avenue, Pratt Station Brooklyn, N.Y. 11205

Please send me the books I have checked above. Orders for less than 5 books must include 60¢ for the first book and 25¢ for each additional book to cover mailing and handling. Postage is FREE for orders of 5 books or more. Check or money order only. Please include sales tax.

Name_____ Books $_____
                                        Postage _____
Address_____ Sales Tax _____
City_____ State/Zip_____ Total $_____

Please allow 4 to 5 weeks for delivery

B-16

WESTERNS

☐ LION OF THE LAVABEDS Walker A. Tompkins	00706-0	.95
☐ THE LONELY LAW Matt Stuart	00434-7	1.25
☐ THE PLUNDERERS L. P. Holmes	00688-9	.95
☐ THE QUIET GUN Leo Brady	08489-8	1.25
☐ SIX GUN OUTCAST Charles N. Heckelmann	04001-7	1.25
☐ THE TRAIL OF THE IRON HORSE Walker A. Tompkins	00704-4	.95
☐ VENGEANCE IS MINE Jed Cross	00685-4	.95
☐ WILD SUMMIT L. P. Holmes	00692-7	.95

Buy them at your local bookstores or use this handy coupon for ordering:

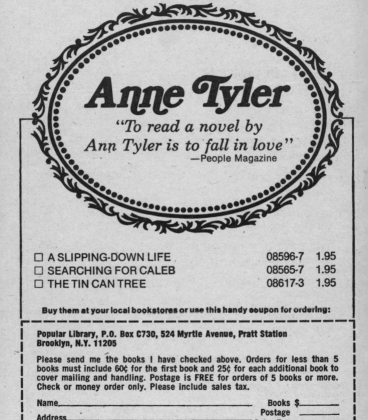

Reading Fit For A Queen

QUEEN-SIZE GOTHICS are a new idea. They offer the very best in novels of romantic suspense, by the top writers, greater in length and drama, richer in reading pleasure.

☐ THE FOUR MARYS—Rinalda Roberts	00366-9	1.25
☐ GRAVE'S COMPANY—S. Nichols	00252-2	1.25
☐ GRENENCOURT—I. Charles	00264-6	1.25
☐ THE HARLAN LEGACY— Jo Anne Creighton	03206-5	1.50
☐ THE HEMLOCK TREE—E. Lottman	00235-2	1.25
☐ ISLAND OF SILENCE— Carolyn Brimley Norris	00411-8	1.25
☐ ISLAND OF THE SEVEN HILLS—Z. Cass	00277-8	1.25
☐ KEYS OF HELL—L. Osborne	00284-0	1.25
☐ THE KEYS TO QUEENSCOURT— Jeanne Hines (Empress)	08508-8	1.75
☐ THE LAZARUS INHERITANCE (Large type)—Noel Vreeland Carter	00432-0	1.25
☐ THE LEGEND OF WITCHWYND (Large type)—Jeanne Hines	00420-7	1.25
☐ LET THE CRAGS COMB OUT HER DAINTY HAIR—J. Marten	00302-2	1.25
☐ LUCIFER WAS TALL—Elizabeth Gresham	00346-4	1.25
☐ MIDNIGHT SAILING—S. Hufford	00263-8	1.25
☐ THE MIRACLE AT ST. BRUNO'S— Philippa Carr (Empress)	08533-9	1.75
☐ OF LOVE INCARNATE—Jane Crowcroft	00418-5	1.25

Buy them at your local bookstores or use this handy coupon for ordering: